Sure, animals are just doing what c_____ but we have to ask: just how *natural* is . . .

- A cat in Florida, choking on her flea collar, steps on the speed-dial button for 911, bringing a police response unit
- Responding to the beep of pocket pagers hung around their necks, cattle in Japan head straight for their feeding station
- Three bottlenose dolphins come to the rescue of a man being attacked by a shark, flapping their fins and tails to frighten the shark until help arrives
- A chimpanzee at the Krakow Zoo chooses stocks on the Warsaw stock exchange and earns a ten-percent return over a three-month period
- Mutant two-foot-long rats made fat by the droppings of hormone-fed poultry go on a rampage in Chile, attacking chickens and small goats

From the orangutan who leaves two tourists naked in the woods to the squirrel who devotes his life to stealing American flags from cemeteries, here are 100 percent true news accounts from the annals of animal antics and misadventures you'll just have to read to believe.

John J. Kohut is a political analyst for a large corporation in Washington, D.C. He has been collecting strange news clippings for more than two decades and is the author of *Stupid Government Tricks*.

Roland Sweet is a magazine editor and writes his own syndicated column. Kohut and Sweet are the authors of *Dumb, Dumber, Dumbest* and, most recently, *More Dumb, Dumber, Dumbest*, both available in Plume editions.

STRANGE TAILS

All-Too-True News from the Animal Kingdom

Collected by
John J. Kohut
and Roland Sweet

A PLUME BOOK

PLUME
Published by the Penguin Group
Penguin Putnam Inc., 375 Hudson Street, New York, New York 10014, U.S.A.
Penguin Books Ltd, 27 Wrights Lane, London W8 5TZ, England
Penguin Books Australia Ltd, Ringwood, Victoria, Australia
Penguin Books Canada Ltd, 10 Alcorn Avenue, Toronto, Ontario, Canada M4V 3B2
Penguin Books (N.Z.) Ltd, 182–190 Wairau Road, Auckland 10, New Zealand

Penguin Books Ltd, Registered Offices:
Harmondsworth, Middlesex, England

First published by Plume, a member of Penguin Putnam Inc.

First Printing, October, 1999
10   9   8   7   6   5   4   3   2   1

 REGISTERED TRADEMARK—MARCA REGISTRADA

LIBRARY OF CONGRESS CATALOGING-IN-PUBLICATION DATA

Strange tails : all-too-true news from the animal kingdom / collected by John J. Kohut and
    Roland Sweet.
        p.   cm.
    Includes bibliographical references.
    ISBN 0-452-28118-0
    1. Animal behavior Anecdotes.   I. Kohut, John J.   II. Sweet, Roland.
QL751.S715   1999
591.5—dc21   99-22281
                                                                         CIP

Printed in the United States of America
Set in Century Book
Designed by Leonard Telesca

In memory of
Zak and Chanel and Attilla and Bandit

🐰 Contents

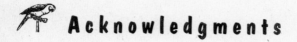 # Acknowledgments

Thanks to Theo for the swell idea.

Thanks to Lisa for her encouragement.

Also, we extend our appreciation and admiration to those resourceful reporters and hard-nosed editors who uncovered these stories in the first place, not to mention the many newspapers, large and small, that saw fit to print them. The papers we used are listed in the back.

Finally, thanks to the many readers of our previous collections of offbeat news (most still affordably in print) for sending us clippings from your local papers. Please continue, but note our new mailing address (as of 1999):

News Quirks
P.O. Box 8130
Alexandria, VA 22306-8130

Incidentally, we are not on the Internet. Thanks for asking.

⼇ Introduction

It may have dawned on you already. We are not alone.

For eons, humans have lived under their gaze. Day and night, they monitor our every move. Watching. Waiting. So much like us and yet, so, well, alien.

What do they want? Usually something to eat. Occasionally us.

Beast or burden, animals are part of human life. Over the years, we've classified them as those fit to share our homes; those best seen in zoos, circuses, or televised nature documentaries; and everything else, which constitutes the actual wild. The animals, in turn, regard us as either useful to their survival, best ignored or avoided, or dangerous encroachers who must be driven out.

After twenty years spent covering the strange-news beat, we've observed that it isn't just people who are weird. Animal oddities also abound. Just consider:

- a squirrel who devotes its life to stealing American flags
- a bear who ambushes cyclists and steals their bikes
- an orangutan who strips the clothes off startled tourists, puts them on himself, and leaves his victims naked in the jungle.

Animals shoot our guns, drive our cars, use our telephones, and pick up some of our worst habits.

And the things people do to them! Small wonder animals sometimes seem to seek revenge.

To show you what we mean, we submit these dispatches from the animal kingdom—five-hundred-plus strange-but-true news stories collected over the past fifteen years—chronicling the antics of animals and the people who interact with them, whether at home, in the wild, or in the science lab. Victim or perpetrator, animals clearly demonstrate that it wouldn't be a weird world without them.

John J. Kohut
Roland Sweet

MONKEYS' UNCLES

Animals Coping with People
and Their World

Quick-Change Artist

While a French tourist was enjoying a walk through a Malaysian ape sanctuary on Borneo island, a 14-year-old male orangutan named Raja grabbed him, pulled off his pants, shirt, and underwear, then fled into the woods with the clothes. "This unusual incident is a warning to all tourists to wear clothes which cannot be removed easily," a park official said, adding that authorities would track Raja "and see if the animal attempts to wear the Frenchman's clothes."

Catchy Tunes

American scientist Dr. Hector Corona announced that dolphins in the wild sing along to the radio. By slowing down recordings of dolphins to one-quarter speed, he discovered that sometimes they are singing popular hits, which they hear by picking up sound waves from radios on boats and beaches.

Vote Getters

• In a 1996 Brazilian municipal election, the leading candidate for mayor of Pilar died mysteriously. Even more mysterious, the front-runner was a goat. The week after a parade of

50 vehicles filled with the goat's supporters came under gunfire, its owner, Petrucio Maia, said he suspected a political rival had poisoned the goat, telling the *Folha de Sao Paulo* newspaper the animal "had a lot a foam in his mouth."

• When Tiao the chimp, a major attraction at the Rio de Janeiro zoo, died, the mayor declared a mourning period of eight days. Tiao also ran for mayor in 1988, representing the Brazilian Bana Party, and placed third with more than 400,000 votes.

Art for Art's Sake

Researchers at Tokyo's Keio University announced they have taught pigeons to distinguish Cubist paintings from Impressionist ones. Psychologist Shingeru Wantanabe reported the birds can correctly identify the Cubist work 90 percent of the time.

Let's See Your License

• A police officer in Uhrichsville, Ohio, followed a pickup truck as it pulled out of a shopping center parking lot after dark without its lights on. The truck turned on a street, ran over a median strip, across a lawn, through a ditch, and into a cornfield. When the truck turned around, the officer observed that the driver was a dog. He watched as the truck entered a second field before it came to a stop after hitting a pole. The owner of the truck explained he found the stray collie-mix and left it in his truck with the engine running while he went shopping.

• St. Joseph, Missouri, police officer Charles Parsons left his black lab in his Bronco at the police department parking lot while he went inside to get his paycheck. The dog knocked the Bronco out of gear and hit the car of another police officer.

• Florida Department of Law Enforcement agents John

Halliday and Tom Colbert spotted a car moving erratically along busy U.S. 19 in Clearwater, Florida, then noticed a three-and-a-half-foot green-and-orange iguana at the steering wheel. "It looked like the iguana was driving," FDLE supervisor Larry Sams told the *Tampa Tribune*. "He had his claws on top of the wheel." The agents followed the car for several miles before pulling it over and finding the car's owner, John Ruppell, slouched down in the seat. They charged him with drunk driving.

Spoilsport

Brazil's environmental protection institute announced it would seek a ban against television commercials for beer and soft drinks in which chimpanzees drive and drink with bikini-clad women. Lilian Daher, spokesperson for the government agency, explained, "Driving a car and drinking beer or soda is not a monkey's natural habitat."

Reach Out and Touch Someone

• After teaching their cocker spaniel to dial 911 in case of an emergency, Bonnie and Tom Robb of Aliso Viejo, California, received a phone bill with $28 in 900-call charges to Sports Pick and the Adult Date Line. When the calls were made, Bonnie Robb insisted, "We know the dog did it because no one else was home. I know he did it."

• When a Thurston County, Washington, emergency operator answered a call but heard only heavy breathing, Sheriff's Deputy Gary Daurelio was dispatched to investigate. He concluded the caller was a 150-pound pig he found alone inside the house. Daurelio said the pig escaped from its backyard pen, pushed open the back door of the house, went inside, knocked over the telephone, and somehow managed to dial 911.

• Police in Redwood City, California, knocked on the door

of Jan Slominski, explaining that they had received a 911 call from the home. Slominski didn't know why, but further investigation found that the family's 50-pound pig had knocked the phone off the hook and stepped on the speed-dial button for 911. "Now the pigs are calling the pigs," police spokesperson Howard Baker said.

• Des Moines, Iowa, hog farmer Dave Rousselow checked his telephone answering machine and heard squeals and snorts. Recognizing the sound, Rousselow went to the hog lot and found a cellular phone he had lost earlier. Apparently one of the hogs had stepped on the phone's redial button and been connected to the answering machine.

• When Tipper, a nine-month-old cat belonging to Gail Curtis of Tampa, Florida, got its flea collar stuck in its mouth and began to choke, it knocked the telephone receiver off its cradle and stepped on the preprogrammed speed-dial button for 911. On the dispatcher's tape of the call, Tipper's choking and meowing are clearly audible. A sheriff's deputy was sent to the home and rescued the cat.

• Carol Galpin's two dogs ransacked her house in Salisbury, England, while she was at work, pulling dozens of books off the shelves and generally wreaking havoc. During their rampage, they dragged Galpin's telephone into her bedroom and onto the bed, then dialed that country's 999 emergency number by pushing the button three times. The dispatcher heard only gurgling and heavy breathing, so she assumed someone was in trouble and alerted police officers. When they saw the destruction, they figured someone had broken into the home, but when Galpin arrived home she theorized the dogs had called the police because "they might've known they'd done something."

• When 911 operators in Wauwatosa, Wisconsin, couldn't hear a voice on the other end of a call, they sent police, paramedics, and the fire department to the address where the call originated. Emergency personnel found no one at home but a basset hound and a partially chewed cordless phone.

• A terrier pup in London named Jemima pulled the telephone off a table while her owner was at work and scratched the 9 button three times. When police arrived at the house and no one answered the door, they assumed the worst and broke down the door.

• Police in Boynton Beach, Florida, responded to a home from which several 911 calls were placed. After the caller failed to talk to the police dispatcher, officers on the scene banged on the door until resident Barbara Marple woke up and answered the door. When she denied making the calls, police said that they wanted to look around. They found Marple's cat in her bedroom with a paw on the cordless telephone and determined that it kept hitting 911 on redial.

Overdomesticated

• A Swedish veterinarian, summoned to a farm at Linkoping to examine 2,500 pigs described as reeling drunk, told the newspaper *Ostgoten* that the farmer had unwittingly fed the swine fermented juice, yogurt, and milk. As a result, he said, they were behaving "just like humans."

• Three sheep and a cow died from an overdose of marijuana in south Brazil. Farmhand Paulo Sergio Goulart told reporters he found bricks of plastic-wrapped cannabis hidden in a pen, thought it was dried alfalfa, and fed it to the animals, who soon began falling down, bleating and mooing. "It was a good thing that the cow wasn't giving milk," he said, "or people would have gotten stoned by just drinking it."

Great Escape

A Russian tourist agent who was asked to provide an American visitor to Russia with a wild bear hunt bought a bear from a circus and released it in Moscow's Perdelkino Forest. The newspaper *Vecernaya Moskva* reported that as the hunter closed in on the prey, a postal carrier on a bicycle passed by, saw the bear, and tumbled over in surprise. The trained bear climbed on the bike and pedaled off, leaving the carrier stranded and the American to sue for fraud.

Welcome Legacies

• A superior court jury in Chatsworth, Georgia, ruled that a six-year-old chow dog named Booger Boy was eligible to receive $400 a month from the dog's late owner's estate. Two other beneficiaries of the will had challenged the dog in court.

• When Margo Lamp of Davenport, Iowa, died in 1990, she left $600,000 to her pet pig, Mr. Pig, and her dog, Calamity Jane. After the dog died, Mr. Pig became the sole beneficiary.

Car before the Horse

Police in the Mexican state of Morelia arrested a horse for kicking a car. Reports said the horse was tied up on a street when it kicked in the headlights and damaged the grill of a car parked next to it.

Eight Lives to Go

Cats living in high-rise apartments and condominiums were identified as being susceptible to High-Rise Syndrome, or HRS, the phenomenon of cats diving off of condo balconies and surviving. Veterinarians note that HRS is caused mostly by cats trying to catch birds and say they survive because their weight and shape let them fall at a top speed of only about 60 miles per hour, compared with about 120 miles per hour for a plummeting human. One case often cited is that of Sabrina, a cat in New York City, who fell 32 stories onto a concrete sidewalk and simply chipped a tooth.

Covering Every Angle

• *Dog World* magazine assigned a reporter to cover the O. J. Simpson murder trial because of the prominence of

Nicole Simpson's pet Akita. The dog was found wandering the neighborhood of the murder scene within minutes of the murder with bloody paws. The magazine's editor said that she believed "there was heightened interest about dogs, particularly Akitas, and their sense of awareness, keen loyalty and popularity" because of the trial.

• Attorney Harold Marsh filed a federal lawsuit on behalf of himself and his miniature black poodle after the dog was ejected from the patio dining section of the Los Angeles restaurant Mezzaluna Cafe, the eatery made famous in the O.J. Simpson murder trial. Ronald Goldman, who was murdered along with Nicole Simpson, worked at the restaurant. Marsh claimed that the restaurant violated his pet's constitutional rights, blaming "those idiot tourists" and "other persons similarly insane" for complaining to the city health department about dogs on the patio.

Don't Be Late

Animals appear to sense when their owners are returning home and actually prepare for the event, according to British biologist Rupert Sheldrake. From 1,500 case studies observing the behavior of pets in homes worldwide, he concluded that 46 percent of the dogs began preparing for their owner's return an hour before they got home. He also saw the phenomenon among cats and birds. Besides becoming visibly agitated, the animals started going to the window to watch for their owner.

Shape Up

Total Dog, a health club for dogs, opened in Los Angeles in 1996, with physical therapists offering massage therapy, treadmills, swim-therapy pools, and an aerobic exercise course featuring ladders and slides. Membership costs up to $800 per year. The company suggests that taking a dog to the gym is safer and nicer than going to a city park.

Penned-In Feeling

• Veterinarians at Canada's Calgary Zoo prescribed Prozac to stop Snowball, a 25-year-old chronically depressed polar bear, from neurotically pacing back and forth in its cage. Comparing the condition to "the obsessive-compulsive behavior of some people who wash their hands over and over again," the zoo also used "environmental enrichment" to help the animal cope and fed the bear fish frozen in blocks of ice so that it would have to work for its food as if it were in the wild.

• When Gus, the polar bear at New York City's Central Park Zoo, grew bored, the zoo spent $25,000 to hire animal behavior expert Tim Desmond to act as a psychoanalyst. Gus's symptoms included a swimming obsession in which he repeatedly swam back and forth in place. Among the solutions tried were increasing interaction with keepers, hiding food, and providing educational toys.

Taste of Freedom

At a Tokyo research center, a 13-year-old chimpanzee who had been taught to use a key to open a padlock, hid a key in her mouth, then used it to open her cage. She also unlocked the cages of another chimp and an orangutan, then opened an outer door of the facility so they could escape.

Smarter Than the Scarecrow

While studying crows in the rain forests of New Caledonia in 1996, New Zealand naturalist Gavin Hunt saw four crows manufacturing tools and 68 others using tools to dig insects out of crevices or as carrying devices. Hunt suggested that the crows were using tools at a skill level on a par with early humans.

It Happens

• Japan's Rony Company announced the invention of a toilet for cats. Costing $1,640, it lets the animals relieve themselves without getting wet, the company claimed, "thanks to an infrared system which starts the flush when the cat leaves and dries the seat for the next one."

• Richard R. Wooten, 37, of Bowie, Maryland, announced he had invented a device that lets dogs use a home's toilet when they have to go. Designed for small dogs whose owners don't like walking them, the lightweight Walk-Me-Not wheels into place over a regular toilet. It has a platform that swings down to be washed with a jet spray after the dog leaves.

Wooten, who's allergic to dogs and whose living room walls display large, framed photographs of small dogs using his invention, said he got his inspiration while stationed in Paris, where everyone has a dog and "there's so much stuff on the ground you can't walk straight." He spent eight years developing the puppy potty, sacrificing a normal life. "I'd like to have a family, have kids, but I don't need the responsibility because I have to do things [for the Walk-Me-Not] at a moment's notice," he said. "I don't want to say 'I can't go to this meeting because I have to take my son to the baseball game.' "

Next They'll Want Cable

• The Twycross, England, zoo announced it would spend $480,000 to build its three gorillas a new play area that includes color television. "They really like the telly," said Molly Badham, the zoo's owner. "When the keeper turns it off they scream."

• A group of battery hens being tested to see whether television images would calm their self-destructive aggressive tendencies became hooked on the images, according to researchers at Scotland's Roslin Institute. "Now, as soon as the TV appears, they whiz across and spend time there," researcher Bryan Jones told *New Scientist* magazine, noting that images of fish and flying toasters had the most calming effect.

• An owl in China's Jiangxi province became addicted to television after it flew into the home of farmer Zhang Liuyou, perched on a beam, and joined the family in viewing the evening's programs. The *China Daily* reported that after returning regularly for the next year, the owl built a nest under the eaves of the house, where it sleeps during the day, coming out at night to watch TV from either the beam or the dining table.

• The *Shanghai Evening News* reported that a dog died while watching a violent TV program. The dog was watching a show with its owner when a scene showed a man with a gun jumping out of some bushes. The dog responded by howling and running around the house frantically. It then began to foam at the mouth, had a heart attack, and died.

Commuter Vehicle

To dramatize traffic congestion in Lisbon, Portugal's Socialist party organized a race between a burro and a Ferrari 348 TS coupe on a 1.6-mile course along a crowded road from suburban Odivelas to one of the main entrances of the capital. The burro beat the Ferrari by four minutes.

When Jolyn Grunts, People Listen

• The *San Francisco Chronicle* picked eight local investment managers in 1993 to select stocks that they thought had superior potential. To introduce a random element, the paper also had Jolyn, an orangutan from Marine World-Africa USA, jab darts at the stock pages. Six of the eight humans beat Standard & Poor's 500 index. Jolyn's picks outperformed two of the humans and the S&P.

• Karolina, a chimpanzee at the Krakow zoo, chose stocks

on the Warsaw stock exchange and earned a 10 percent return on investment over a three-month period in 1996—better than the investments made by a local brokerage firm. Karolina chose five tangerines from a bunch of more than 70, each bearing the name of a firm considered for investment. Some analysts did outperform the chimp, but Karolina also beat the return on treasury bonds and the dollar during the same time period.

Toasted

Officials at the Copenhagen Zoo announced that one of its okapis had died from stress, apparently caused by opera singers rehearsing Wagner's *Tannhauser* in a park 300 yards away. After its death, the rare African mammal was sent to Copenhagen University's zoological museum to be stuffed, but students reportedly skinned the corpse, then cooked and ate the meat.

Planet of the Apes

• Scientists launched a global campaign to have the United Nations declare gorillas, chimpanzees, and orangutans equal to human beings. Inspired by English philosopher Peter Singer, the Declaration on Great Apes guarantees the animals right to life, protection of individual liberty, and freedom from torture. "This goes further than animal welfare," Singer said. "This recognizes them as nonhuman persons who are not property but individuals in their own right."

• Sue Savage-Rumbaugh, a Georgia State University psychologist who pioneered research into apes' language ability, said that gorillas, chimpanzees, and other apes deserve at least the same protection as severely retarded children. "We certainly would not put these children in a zoo to be gawked at as examples of nature," she explained, announcing support for the Great Ape Movement to grant apes semi-human legal status.

Naughty Noises

Ernest and Frances Haskins complained to a British court that they were kept awake at night because their neighbor's rabbits made too much noise mating. The court ruled that they did not have to hear the cavorting animals' constant "scratching, thumping, and banging," prompting the rabbits' owner, Joyce Hartley, to agree to build a garden shed to muffle their amorous sounds.

See If Anyone Salutes

Authorities investigating the thefts of American flags from graves in Wellsboro, Pennsylvania, determined that the culprit was a squirrel. Witnesses said the animal jumped down from a tree, grabbed a flag, and stripped it from its pole, then ran back up the tree carrying the flag.

Song in the Air

• Blackbirds in the English town of Gulsborough began imitating the wailing sirens of car alarms. The noise regularly awakens townspeople, reported bartender Donald O'Shea, who said he discovered the phenomenon when he rushed out at dawn to confront car thieves but found only a bird in mid-song.

• Traffic noise is causing songbirds living near busy highways to lose their ability to produce calls, according to the British Ecological Society. It found that birds are so off-key that they cannot warn intruders to leave their territory or attract a mate, adding that courting calls of birds living within two or three miles of major highways cannot be heard by prospective partners.

Picky, Picky, Picky

To feed bald eagles at the Rocky Mountain Arsenal in Colorado, the U.S. Fish and Wildlife Service began collecting mule deer that had been killed on highways. Shortly after starting the program, the agency reported it was swamped with dead deer because the finicky eagles refused to eat the roadkill.

Underground Nature

• Pigeons ride the London subway, judging from letters responding to a query by the magazine *New Scientist*. Readers indicated that the birds seem to know where they are going, which lines to take, and when to get off. Lorna Read wrote: "A pigeon, calm as you please, hopped on my Northern Line carriage at King's Cross and stood quite calmly near the door. It appeared to know where it was going as soon as the doors opened at Euston, where it flew out."

• London's subway also appears to be the breeding ground for a new type of mosquito that has adapted to life below the surface. Kate Byrne, a population geneticist at London University's Queen Mary and Westfield College, explained that the mosquitoes probably evolved from ones that became trapped when the tunnels were dug a century ago. Since then, the subway's warm and damp conditions have fostered the growth of the mosquitoes, which suck the blood of rats, mice, and humans. Although scientists stopped short of calling the mosquito, dubbed "molestus," a new species, they noted that attempts to breed them with surface-raised mosquitoes failed. They also have characteristics unique to their respective subway lines.

• Rats invaded a sewer system in the Ukraine and began using it as a "sort of subway for rats," a local official said, to sneak into homes through the toilets. The newspaper *Daily Express* reported that one elderly woman in Dnipropetrovsk died of shock after finding a sopping rat in her toilet bowl.

Overdomesticated

The plight of alcoholic donkeys in England moved Dr. Elisabeth Svendsen to open a retreat where they can sober up. Explaining that the usually docile animals turn aggressive after their owners introduce them to drink, she noted one donkey, which had been trained to pick up a half-pint of beer with its lips and drink it in one gulp, ended up attacking the owner's wife. "We had a group of three donkeys who came in here from a pub that was closed down," Svendsen said. "They had been fed on Guinness and potato chips."

We Got Next

Finnish researchers announced success teaching rats to play basketball. Psychologist Sini Paananen trained two rats to snatch the nut-filled ball from one another, scamper to the end of a court, and dunk the ball. Every time they scored, they got a scrap of food.

Animal Lovers

• Florida's Department of Natural Resources recommended banning tourist attractions where customers pay to get into the water with captive bottle-nosed dolphins because adult males sometimes become sexually aroused and make sexual overtures to humans, including physical aggression and other aspects of their aquatic mating ritual. In one incident, a Miami legal secretary reported that soon after she entered the water, she noticed one of the dolphins rubbing against her in an unmistakably amorous way. "He liked me a lot," she recalled. Suddenly the 700-pound animal spun her in the water and swam across her back. "I'm going, 'What the hell's going on? Get him away from me!' I was really scared."

• British police announced they were seeking a man who was seen touching the genitals of a 12-foot bottle-nosed dolphin off the pier at the fishing village of Amble, Northumberland, in what they believe to be the first incident of a sexual assault on a dolphin. "There are several people involved," said marine zoologist Peter Bloom, who has seen injuries on the dolphin's penis that he concluded are the result of people encouraging the animal to use the organ unnaturally. "It's an increasing problem with tame dolphins in the wild. In Dingle Bay [Ireland] a few weeks ago I saw a stark-naked woman running into the sea shouting, 'Come on, Fungie, I love you.' Dolphins bring out the best and the worst in people."

We Gotta Get Out of This Place

In Inner Mongolia, 530 sheep and goats tried to commit suicide by jumping into a lake. China's Xinhua news agency reported that 20 herdsmen managed to save 281 of the animals during a three-hour rescue effort, which was hampered when some animals who had been pulled to shore tried to jump back in the water.

Listen Closely

Thinking they heard a child in danger, police in Genoa, Italy, broke into an apartment, only to discover a bird singing, "Mama, mama, help!" The bird, an Indian song thrush whose owner had taught it to speak, was startled by the door being broken down but soon resumed singing, "Mama, mama, help!"

Watchdogs

To slow rush-hour commuter traffic through the Dutch city of Culemborg, head of maintenance Henk-Jan Kievit, 33, instituted a pilot program to station six sheep at intersections in a three-block area in the Goilberdingen neighborhood. The city council said that if the program succeeded, it would consider turning more sheep loose along major routes.

Kicks Just Keep Getting Harder to Find

The Barcelona soccer club presented a ball signed by all its players to Copito de Nieve, an albino gorilla in the city zoo, to mark the thirtieth anniversary of the animal's arrival.

Good-bye Cruel World

Some 225 walruses tried to waddle to their death at Alaska's Togiak National Wildlife Refuge. Wildlife officials reported that although they were able to divert 155 of the marine mammals, 70 others tumbled from a 200-foot cliff above their normal resting beach.

Brainstorm

A Dutch rubber factory began producing water beds for cows. The water-filled rubber mats cost $175 each. "It is good for a cow to lie comfortably," Ton Broere, a salesperson at the Dunlop-Enerka factory in Drachten told the daily *De Voilkskrant.* "Then she will produce more milk."

Litigating Nature

Kim Novacs of Jupiter, Florida, announced she was suing alligators for $1 million. And she expected the state Game and Freshwater Fish Commission to pay on their behalf. Noting the suit was prompted by the state's charging her husband with killing an alligator that threatened their daughter, Novacs explained that if animals protected under the federal Endangered Species Act have the right to sue, then the reverse must be true: People should be allowed to sue a protected animal if it causes harm.

The Velvet Frog

Henry Kissinger disclosed that his baritone voice disturbed the frogs while he was staying at the exclusive Bohemian Grove in California. The frogs set up such a racket that a herpetologist was called in to tape Kissinger talking. The tape also caused the frogs to go berserk. The best explanation that could be offered was that the statesman's voice resembled that of a male frog in heat.

Turn on C-SPAN

Veterinarians at the Warsaw zoo, concerned that their chimpanzees were suffering from the winter blahs, recommended that the primates watch television for three hours a day. "They have ropes, tires, a hammock, and old clothes to tear up," said Ewa Zbonikowska, "but they get bored with all of it after a while this time of year."

Hooked on Toil

Elephants used in illegal logging operations in northern Thailand's Mae Riang-Soi Yaeng forest reserve are fed amphetamine-laced bananas to speed up their work, the *Bangkok Post* reported. At least 10 of the animals died of overwork and exhaustion as a result, according to Dr. Preecha Puangkham, a volunteer at the Lampang province elephant hospital, which has treated several elephants for amphetamine addiction.

Back to the Drawing Board

Japan's first effort to send a rocket to the moon was delayed when the nation's space agency had to curtail engine tests on the island of Hokkaido after the noise startled 500 chickens, causing them to stampede and smash themselves to death against a henhouse wall. According to the *Washington Post*, the National Space Development Agency apologized to local chicken farmers and announced it would move the tests to another site, despite the time and money involved.

Art Smart

Researchers at the National Institutes of Health Animal Center gave clay spheres, stones, paint, and leaves to 10 capuchin monkeys. Within 30 minutes, the monkeys had reshaped the clay with their hands and decorated it with paint and leaves. According to *New Scientist* magazine, the animals may have awakened their creative urge by not having to spend time hunting for food or looking out for predators. "They were very focused when they were making them," researcher Gregory Westergaard said. "Art doesn't happen unless you are smart, and I think such expressions are the inevitable consequence of an intelligent but restless mind."

If Pigs Could Vote

Mariann Fischer Boels, campaigning for reelection to the Danish parliament, proposed giving the country's 11 million pigs toys to play with. Fischer Boels's offer was aimed at the growing environmental and animal rights lobby in Denmark, which has twice as many pigs as people.

Bird on Hand

Richard Stone, 58, was tending his vegetable garden in Cheddar, England, when his van rolled forward and pinned him to the ground. His cries for help went unanswered until a red, blue, and green macaw parrot named Sonny heard him from its cage in a nearby trailer park and imitated him. Two passers-by heard the parrot, investigated, and freed Stone.

Feline Fetishist

A cat in Wellington, New Zealand, was caught stealing women's underwear. Reuters reported the tomcat collected some 60 bras and slips on its nightly travels.

Arnold Ziffel's Web Site

Pigs can be taught to use computers to communicate with humans, according to Penn State University professor Stanley Curtis. He said his experiments involved teaching pigs to use their snouts and mouths to manipulate joysticks to move a circle around a computer screen, trying to put it on a blue target. Curtis insisted that the goal of his research is to provide the best environment for pigs and other farm animals.

Scout's Honor

When Joan Hemmer saw a chimpanzee dressed as a Boy Scout walking into Fricke's Old Hook Inn in Freehold, New Jersey, where she was dining, she said the sight "scared the wits" out of her, causing her to bump into a wall and reinjure her shoulder. She sued the chimp's owner, Ronald Winters. He told the jury that the animal, named Mr. Jiggs, had lived a domesticated life since being taken from the jungle at age six months and was now living in a house and able to feed and clean up after himself. What's more, he said, Mr. Jiggs had entered the restaurant on his way to entertain at a Boy Scout troop banquet. The jury sided with Mr. Jiggs.

Udder Disaster

When a farmworker left a loaded rifle in a field near Velez, Colombia, a cow stepped on the trigger, firing a bullet into the head of another cow grazing nearby.

WILD THINGS

Animals Just Following
Their Instincts

Love Is Blind

• A 700-pound bull moose lumbered into a yard in Waterboro, Maine, and mounted a plastic foam deer used for archery practice. The moose continued its mating attempt until the deer's head fell off, then wandered off in apparent confusion.

• Marge Alvarez was walking through a safari park near Mexico City when an alligator tried to mate with her alligator-hide boots. Park wardens fired a tranquilizer dart at the reptile but missed and had to resort to using a fire hose to chase it away. "I've seen alligators do strange things," park warden Raphael Gonzalez said, "but this beats all."

• Patricia Wyatt called police in Key West, Florida, to report a stray potbellied pig courting her husband's brand-new Harley-Davidson. While trying to have sex with the motorcycle's front wheel, the 50-pound pig scratched the paint and tore the bike's fabric cover, causing at least $100 damage. Animal control officers said the unclaimed stray would be neutered, but the bike's owner, Walter Wyatt, protested the punishment. "His crime is an alleged sex act against a Harley," Wyatt said. "We don't even know if that's a felony."

• A 13-foot whale fell in love with the Norwegian ferry *Voksa*. Witnesses said that the whale was apparently attracted by the ferry's black and white color markings and that it regularly bumped into it, a sign of whale courtship ritual.

• Another whale, a 50-footer off Norway's western coast, was smitten by a 34-foot fishing boat and began rubbing itself alongside the vessel. Fisherman Sverre Klern had to start his boat and sail away. "I've never seen anything like it," he said, "and I started fishing as a small boy."

Bovine Smorgasbord

Thirty-two cows on Bobby and Judy Odermann's dairy farm in Olympia, Washington, ate themselves to death after one of them shook loose a pipe on an automatic feeding machine, releasing tons of grain. "A cow will eat grain until it dies," veterinarian Dr. Michael Paros explained. "They just don't know any better."

Kon-Tiki Revisited

At least 15 green iguanas traveled about 150 miles from Guadeloupe to Anguilla on a raft of logs after Hurricanes Luis and Marilyn blew through the Caribbean in September 1995. The species hadn't previously lived on Anguilla, according to Ellen Censky of Pittsburgh's Carnegie Museum of Natural History, who said local fishermen reported seeing the animals on the beach after the raft washed up there. Censky and her colleagues said the iguanas represented the first convincing evidence that animal voyagers could start a new population when they reach land.

Good News, Bad News

Ornithologists were elated by the sighting beside a road in Australia's Queensland state of an elusive night parrot thought to be extinct, having not been seen in nearly 80 years. Their joy was tempered by the fact that the emerald green and yellow-spotted bird was dead, the likely victim of a car's windshield.

Something Fishy

Park officials in the Chicago suburb of Glen Ellyn, Illinois, reported that a picturesque lake was being choked by goldfish apparently dumped there by pet owners. The officials said the lake, which had no goldfish five years before, now has 350,000 of the fast-reproducing fish.

Amscray

After residents of fashionable neighborhoods on South Africa's Cape Peninsula complained that scores of jackass penguins had invaded their neighborhood, street cleaners climbed through thick brush to remove some 200 of the birds from their hiding places. The penguin colony, which grew from two pairs brought to the area in 1982, had become a popular tourist attraction by 1997, although their noise and smelly droppings made them less welcome with residents.

Crypto Pets

• Two years and four months after the Cummins family of Edmonton, Alberta, lost their pet hamster, it turned up alive— living in the sofa. According to the *Victoria Times-Colonist*, the rodent apparently burrowed into the stuffing, lived off scraps left by the family's other pets, and drank water from the cat's bowl at night. Meanwhile, the family had moved twice since the hamster's disappearance.

• After Rebecca Hampton moved her family from Oklahoma to Rhode Island, she believed that the family cat, Simon, had been lost. Actually Simon was caught under a box spring when the movers were packing up the house in Oklahoma and was trapped in a moving crate for 22 days with no food or water. When her husband opened the crate in Rhode Island, he found Simon, hungry and dehydrated but alive.

More Cause to Worry

A predator fish that suddenly and mysteriously appeared in rivers and streams in western Ukraine began rapidly consuming all other marine life, according to the Itar-Tass news agency. When local fishermen tried to test the fish's ability to survive, they pulled a few of them from the water and left them in the open air. The next day, they threw the fish into an aquarium, where they revived. The agency reported that the fish that regained control of its body first ate up the rest.

Cure Worse Than the Disease

The rats that consume one-third of Tanzania's corn crop were significantly reduced by the recent arrival of red-and-black snakes. Trouble is, the farmers were so frightened by the snakes, which measure up to 13 feet long and coil around cornstalks waiting to attack the rodents, that many began setting fires around their property to keep out the snakes, even at the risk of losing their crops to rats.

Street-Fighting Ram

Traffic was tied up in Cairo, Egypt, when two rams destined for slaughter took an instant dislike to each other and began fighting in the street. The *Al-Gumhuriya* newspaper reported that as motorists stopped to watch, the animals' owner tried to separate the battling rams, only to be thrown to the ground by the rams before traffic police finally subdued them.

Hands Off

Australia's Queensland state issued an official Workplace Health and Safety guide especially prepared for professional crocodile handlers that advised them, among other things, not to "place any part of one's body in the mouth of a crocodile." Written for the state's burgeoning crocodile industry, including 17 game farms and parks, the government-published guide also mentioned the occupational hazards of collecting crocodile eggs, "show" feeding, and capturing adult crocs—especially if the boat is smaller than the reptile. Under the heading "Unsafe Activities," the guide further warns: "Do not sit on the back of a crocodile."

Oldest Profession

Scientists at the South Pole found that female penguins make males pay to have sex with them. Payment is in the form of stones, which the females need for nest platforms. The researchers on Antarctica's Ross Island observed that paired females sneak away from their mates and approach the nests of unpaired males. After mating, the female grabs a stone to take back to her nest. Sometimes merely flirting with the single males will win females a stone.

The Ears Have It

Researchers at England's Cambridge University concluded that prehistoric animals breathed through their ears.

Just Being Fruitful

Officials in the Australian state of Victoria announced that the government was offering prizes to hunters who turn in fox scalps. Foxes, brought to Australia in the nineteenth century and bred for hunting, now number three million and are killing off native species that they prey on. Under the eradication program, dubbed "Foxlotto," hunters receive lottery tickets good for resort holidays, dinners, and sporting goods.

Lather-Stocking Tales

After Starkville, Mississippi, found itself beset by as many as seven million blackbirds, aldermen proposed solving the problem by hiring a plane to fly over the pine woods where the birds roost at night and spray them with liquid detergent. The lawmakers reasoned that when the next rain fell, the water would combine with the detergent to remove the oil from the birds' feathers, causing them to freeze to death.

Stentorian Defense

Svein Harald Folleraas, deputy mayor of the southern Norwegian village of Songdalen, was hunting rabbits when he was charged by a moose protecting her young. "I unleashed a tremendous shout," the politician told the Oslo newspaper *Verdens Gang.* "The moose instantly collapsed onto the ground, a meter from me." After a few seconds, the stunned moose staggered to its feet and wobbled quietly away, according to the newspaper, which reported that witnesses corroborated Folleraas's account.

Rescue Me

• Martin Richardson was swimming in the Red Sea off Egypt's Sinai Peninsula when a shark attacked, taking bites out of his side and arm. As he screamed, three bottle-nosed dolphins circled the man, flapping their fins and tails to frighten away the shark. The dolphins continued circling until Richardson's companions reached him by boat.

• Five survivors of a shipwreck off the Philippines floated on a makeshift raft for three days before a giant sea turtle came by. After they managed to tie the raft to one of the turtle's legs, the turtle towed them for two hours to where fishermen spotted the survivors.

• When Lottie Stevens, 18, washed up on the shore in New Caledonia 17 days after his boat capsized, he said he floated on the overturned boat for four days before trying to swim to safety. He claimed that a stingray then appeared and carried him on its back for 450 miles over 13 days before reaching land.

Grin and Bear It

Pilot Dave Brownlee and biologist John Paczkowski were flying at a low altitude over Kananaskis Park in Canada's Alberta province tracking a grizzly bear fitted with a radio collar when their small plane lost power and crashed. The two were unhurt but had to take refuge in a tree when the bear gave chase.

Save Your Sympathy

Six razor-toothed piranhas at a British aquarium were no match for an eight-pound trout that jumped from a neighboring tank and ate them all. Despite their reputation as the world's most ferocious freshwater fish, "piranha are small fish and would have been stunned by a whopping trout landing in their midst," said a spokesman for the Federation of British Aquatic Societies, insisting, "They can be surprisingly timid."

Two for the Price of One

A seven-year-old billy goat in Culin, France, became a local celebrity by fathering baby goats for four straight years, then suckling three or four each year. His owner, Albert Goyet, said the goat would be a perfect mother if he could only bear young, "which is not the case." Goyet said the 220-pound ram is "not effeminate" and has the "normal feistiness" of any male, adding he lets the goat nurse the kids since he "cannot reconcile himself to milking a billy goat."

Bad Habits

Rangers at Grand Canyon National Park in Arizona began killing mule deer who had become so addicted to junk food left by visitors that they had lost their natural ability to digest vegetation. Explaining that two dozen of the deer would be killed because they are "almost starving to death," park official David Haskell called junk food the "crack cocaine of the deer world."

Because They're There

The Union Electric Company of St. Louis announced that it would pay the World Bird Sanctuary $25,000 for a two-year study to learn why woodpeckers prefer to live, eat, and store their belongings in utility poles.

Uh-oh

Officials in China reported that pandas in Sichuan province are turning from their traditionally exclusive diet of bamboo to eating sheep. According to the state-run Xinhua News Agency, the pandas devoured 48 sheep in just one year in two villages.

Something for Nothing

According to Mackay Consultants of Inverness, Scotland's Loch Ness monster is an industry worth $42 million a year—even though there is no scientific proof that it exists. A half-million tourists visit the Scottish lake each year hoping to see the creature, creating about 2,500 jobs.

Handy Habitat

Harvard University entomologist E. O. Wilson reported discovering a previously unknown species of ant. He found it living in a potted plant on the desk of U.S. World Wildlife Fund president Kathryn Fuller.

Hefty Prey

After spending eight hours trying to rescue a black bear perched 50 to 60 feet up a pine tree near Shreveport, Louisiana, sheriff's deputies, game wardens, and wildlife biologists discovered they had been trying to tranquilize a tattered plastic garbage bag that had caught on a branch.

Dog's Worst Friend

The French owner of a Belgian sheepdog left the animal with relatives to be trained, but it escaped and made its way across more than 600 miles of unfamiliar territory to find its way home. Even though the dog's owner said he was "very moved" by the dog's exploit, a few months later he left the dog with a friend "for the weekend" and he never returned.

Try Again in a Century or Two

After years of encouragement by conservationists, thousands of flamingos returned to a Spanish nature reserve in 1992 to breed for the first time in centuries. But before their eggs could hatch, they were frightened away by firefighting aircraft that accidentally flew low over the restricted area scooping up water. "Within hours, the dozens of eggs left behind were attacked by gulls," said Alberto Martinez, director of the national park.

Down the Drain

Animals topped the list of "Most Unusual Items Found in Sewer and Drain Pipes," compiled by Roto-Rooter, among them birds, bats, beavers, assorted rodents and reptiles, and a 60-pound pig. Other weird drain-stoppers turned up by the survey of 204 Roto-Rooter workers included dentures, glass eyes, gold teeth, hearing aids, toupees, a hockey stick, garden hose, and hummingbird feeder.

Lebensraum

Rhinos, hippos, and elephants should be allowed to die out to make way for grazing land for domestic animals, according to soil expert Munro Munnik of the University of South Africa. Arguing that the wild animals serve no useful purpose and that conservation efforts on their behalf are "unrealistic," Munnik said scientists should "start immediately to plan how to use all natural resources for the benefit of mankind."

Cruel to Be Kind

In England, Judge Alexander Butterfield ordered Jean Knowlson, 68, imprisoned for eight weeks for violating a court order not to feed birds in her yard. Butterfield said the dramatic increase in the pigeon population around her home was the result of her feeding the birds up to 100 loaves of bread a week.

Earth-Shaking Discovery

Jim Berkland, a geologist in Santa Clara County, California, predicted the 1989 Lomo Prieta earthquake by combining statistics on tidal height, positions of the sun, moon, and earth—but mostly by the number of lost cat ads in local papers. Berkland says that for the past decade he has noticed that cats tend to vanish just before a major tremor.

Twice the Fun

Miami University biologists Richard Torkaz and Joseph Slowinski discovered that male lizards, which have two penises, alternate their use to make sure the one they use has the most sperm possible to increase the likelihood of impregnating females. By alternating their penises, the lizards also can copulate frequently without risking a drop in sperm.

New Hope for Weenies

Scientists at Great Britain's Natural Environment Research Council laboratories in Plymouth found that tributyltin (TBT) pollution affects the dog whelk, a shellfish common on British beaches between high-tide and low-tide marks by causing females to grow penises and develop sperm ducts. So many have undergone this transformation that the whelks have been unable to reproduce and are dying out. The scientists reported that their experiment showed the more TBT the females are exposed to, the longer their new penises grow.

Is That a Python in Your Pocket, or Are You Just Glad to See Me?

• The Society for the Prevention of Cruelty to Animals requested that the Malaysian news media carry more "positive reports" about pythons. The group complained that ever since the media reported that a 23-foot python killed and then tried to swallow a 29-year-old rubber plantation worker in Johor state, Malaysians had been indiscriminately killing any snakes they encountered.

• Monsoon floods in Thailand drove phythons from their holes into city streets. During a three-week period, authorities captured almost 100 pythons around Bangkok, according to the director of the Dusit Zoo, Alongkorn Mahannop, who warned, "The big ones can eat people."

Rodney Cow

When a cow wandered onto a freeway in Irvine, California, police in patrol cars tried to herd the animal to an exit, but it panicked and stampeded toward oncoming traffic. Considering the cow a danger to motorists, the officers opened fire, shooting it 43 times before killing it. A police spokesperson said he was at a loss to explain why so many shots were required or where the cow came from, since there are no farms in the Los Angeles suburb.

Fur-Lined Intruders

Phantom Russian submarines that Sweden accused of snooping in its waters during the cold war may actually have been minks, according to a Defense Ministry report to the cabinet. From 1981, when the hunt began, through 1992, Sweden spent $480 million looking for foreign submarines, committing ships, patrol boats, surveillance planes, helicopters with sonar probes, commandos in rubber rafts or kayaks, divers and guards with night-vision equipment, and frequently detonating depth charges to force the intruders to the surface. No intruder was ever found, and none of the suspicious activity was ever traced to foreign intruders. The new report pointed out that minks and some other aquatic animals produce the same sound patterns as submarines when detected by hydrophonic instruments.

Catch-22

Noting that the once-abundant white abalone was virtually wiped out by a commercial harvesting boom in the 1970s as its prized meat fetched high prices, biologists in Ventura, California, reported that after a two-year search, they finally managed to locate three of the mollusks. All were male. Gary Davis, a research biologist with the National Biological Service, explained that researchers trying to save the species cannot afford the extensive search required to find a female, if there even is one, without a grant, and they cannot get a grant until they have a breeding pair.

Return Policy

• Tom Murphy of Pittsburgh sold two of his homing pigeons to buyers in Amarillo and Austin, Texas. A month later, the two birds escaped and flew back to Murphy, making the 1,500-mile flight in five days.

• During a race from Scotland to Wales, a two-year-old British racing pigeon lost its bearings, crossed the North Sea, and wound up in Norway, some 800 miles away. A Norwegian pigeon enthusiast found the bird and contacted its owner, Robert Jones, whose name was on the bird's tag. Jones told him to keep the bird because she was too far away to return. Two months later, however, the bird appeared so homesick that the Norwegian released her. A few days later, the bird arrived safely home.

• In Australia, 8,100 pigeons were released from Hay, New South Wales, for a 340-mile race to Sydney. The race should have taken six hours, but the first birds didn't arrive until the following day. A week later, about one-third of the birds had arrived. The rest never showed up. Sam Beggs, director of the Australian Pigeon Fanciers Association, commented, "I have had 61 years of experience with racing pigeons and I have never seen anything like this before."

• Some 2,400 homing pigeons disappeared during two long-distance races on the same day. About 1,800 pigeons out of 2,000 vanished in a 200-mile race from northern Virginia to central Pennsylvania, while 600 out of 800 birds disappeared during a separate 150-mile race from western Pennsylvania to Philadelphia.

• Ireland's pigeon-racing enthusiasts complained that their birds are going missing, adding they suspect mobile phones may be disrupting the birds' homing instincts. "Pigeons navigate through using the sun and the magnetic fields of the earth," Tony Kehoe, president of one pigeon-racing club told the *Irish Times*. "There may be a problem with mobile phones, there's so much equipment going through the air now."

• Dead pigeons were found strewn along roadsides in France when tens of thousands of pigeons became disoriented after crossing the English Channel to mark the British Racing Pigeon Society's centenary. Laurent Toussaint, in charge of monitoring the race, told the *Times* of London, "There was a magnetic front south of the release point, over the Loire, which would certainly have disoriented them."

It Doesn't Always Come Naturally

Marine biologists and park rangers at a nature preserve off the California coast reported they were on the lookout for an amorous male sea lion nicknamed the "Marauder of San Miguel Island." The 1,800-pound male, a rare hybrid giant that scientists described as a freak of nature, is believed to have killed up to 50 female sea lions a year over a five-year period by crushing them to death with his inept mating attempts.

Snake Eyes

A snake charmer at a house in the Tamil Nadu village of Valangaiman caught a cobra with a hood that looked like a human face. The snake had two dots resembling eyes and a mark for an eyebrow along with marks for a nose and a mouth. Crowds gathered to see the snake, with some worshipping it.

Everybody's a Winner

A fish vendor in Turbo, Colombia, was cleaning fish when he found one with the number 1124 written on its side in paint. After a local radio station reported the find, hundreds of people played the number in the national lottery. The winning number was 1124, and about 300 street vendors and fishermen were among the winners.

Private Sector

Beavers succeeded in building a dam on Oklahoma's Eagle Chief Creek after one built by the U.S. Fish and Wildlife Service washed out in the first big rainstorm. "The beavers have done a better job building a dam than the government did," said the mayor of Avard, Oklahoma.

Honey, I'm Home

Trish and Vincent Caminiti of Bayport, New York, returned from a three-week vacation to find that 20,000 bees had established a hive in the walls of their home. Beekeepers successfully vacuumed the bees out but discovered that they had already produced about four pounds of honey and had 10,000 young bees in development. According to neighbors, the swarm arrived in a dense, black, 10-foot-wide funnel cloud that buzzed so loud some thought it was an aircraft. The swarm then entered the home one at a time through a hole only a half-inch in diameter in the wall of the house.

Bad Hair Day

Mychal Limric, a television-news reporter in Kennewick, Washington, was doing a story on beekeeping when a swarm of bees attacked his head, stinging him about 30 times. Experts concluded the bees were attracted by Limric's hair gel.

Behind the Scenes

Scientists announced in 1995 that they had finally determined the reason for the bizarre incident on which Alfred Hitchcock based his movie *The Birds*. In 1961 flocks of seabirds flew out of a fog bank and attacked the coastal town of Monterey Bay, California. The birds wreaked havoc in the town, running into cars and swarming over buildings, telephone wires, and lampposts. Scientists explained that the birds acted so erratically because they were suffering from food poisoning caused by plankton they had ingested.

Driven Batty

Thousands of bats descended on Sandi and Terry Dowdy's house in Tivoli, Texas, and took up residence in the attic. Terry Dowdy said that after dark the bats leave in groups of 15 or 20 to forage for food. When they return, they often hit the windows and sides of the house trying to get back inside.

Dog Gone

• A crown eagle carried off a Jack Russell terrier puppy from a backyard in Pletermaritzburg, South Africa, but about 15 feet up the puppy got free of the talons and plunged into a swimming pool.

• In Valdez, Alaska, a bald eagle swooped down at a gas station where a motor home was being serviced and made off with the owners' small Chihuahua-like dog, which had been let out to run around. According to witnesses, while the woman was inconsolable at her pet's demise, her husband was on the other side of the camper clapping his hands in the air and saying, "Yeah! Yeah!"

Road Rage

• A raccoon riding on a garbage truck jumped off onto a pickup truck, shattering the windshield and knocking driver John David Antienowicz, 39, unconscious. The *Daytona Beach News-Journal* reported that the driver's 19-year-old son, David Antienowicz, grabbed the wheel and steered the pickup to a stop.

• Anthony Gagliardi, 36, of Havertown, Pennsylvania, was riding his motorcycle along Route 926 when a deer standing on an embankment about seven feet up off the side of the road suddenly leapt onto the man and his motorcycle, landing in his lap and causing a crash. The deer got up and ran away, but Gagliardi died.

• Chris Balsbaugh was parked at a traffic light in Fairfax County, Virginia, with her Great Dane, Rocky, who was sitting in the backseat with the windows down. A pickup truck pulled alongside at the light, and a pit bull riding in the back of the truck suddenly jumped into Balsbaugh's car and attacked Rocky. The two drivers were able to get the dogs out of the car, but then the Great Dane ran down the highway with the pit bull in pursuit. The two drivers caught up with the dogs about a half mile away, where they finally separated the two.

When Elephants Attack

• A herd of migrating elephants in India delayed their search for food by breaking into an Indian Army camp in West Bengal and stealing the soldiers' rum. According to the *New Delhi Statesman*, the elephants liked it so much that they keep coming back for more. The camp tried electric fences and bonfires to keep the herd out, but the animals learned to use their trunks to hose out the fires and to demolish the fences with wooden logs. Once inside the camp, they break open the rum bottles, drink their fill, and stagger back into the forest.

• In India's eastern state of Assam, rampaging elephants killed at least 31 people during attacks on villages. State wildlife Warden H. C. Changkakati explained that some of the attacks came after elephants seeking food broke into stores of rice beer.

• A herd of 45 elephants in search of water happened instead upon six illegal breweries southwest of Calcutta, which they proceeded to destroy and drink in a two-day rampage. Once finished, the drunk elephants were seen stumbling back into the woods. "They are notoriously famous for their fondness for liquor," a forest officer said, "and are great guzzlers."

• One particular elephant in the Indian state of Bihar

became so addicted to alcohol that it regularly visits villages where there are illegal breweries, smashes stills, and drinks the liquor. Once drunk, it would go on a rampage looking for more. Local villagers refer to the elephant as "the excise commissioner."

• Villagers in Handapanagala, Sri Lanka, have spent years hiding in their homes at night for fear of being killed by a herd of elephants that regularly raids villages at night looking for food. In 1995 and 1996 the herd of about 130 elephants killed 70 people. The problem stems from the government's decision in 1986 to clear a large area of jungle and plant thousands of acres of sugarcane. The crop is protected by a 135-mile electric fence, which also cut the elephants' migration route and left the 130 trapped in Handapanagala.

• The Oriental Insurance Company of India began offering group insurance for elephants to pay for cremation in event of death and for tranquilization in event of rampages.

• A herd of more than 1,000 marauding elephants destroyed 11 villages in northern Cameroon, leaving at least four people dead, 375 people homeless, and thousands of acres of crops ruined.

• Although villagers in Nepal lit fires and torches and set off firecrackers to drive away rampaging elephants, seven of them pulled down one man's house and ate 15,000 rupees in cash that he kept in a rice bag. About 2,000 of the rupees ($40) were later found in elephant dung.

In Touch with Their Inner Still

African elephants are renowned for raiding stills to get at alcoholic beverages, but keepers at the Kruger National Park reported that the animals are able to make their own hooch. They stuff themselves with fruit from the marula tree, drink large amounts of water, then walk around to start the fermentation process. Once the concoction turns to alcohol, the beasts stagger all over the park.

ANIMAL HUSBANDRY
The Things People Do to or with Animals

Beeping Bovines

Researchers at Japan's Prefectural Animal Husbandry Experiment Station began teaching cattle to respond to the beep of pocket pagers hung around the animals' necks so they will head for their feeding station with just a phone call instead of having to be rounded up.

Giant Leap for Frogkind

Scientists succeeded in making a frog float in midair. The magazine *New Scientist* reported that the researchers at Britain's University of Nottingham and the University of Nijmegen in the Netherlands also made plants, grasshoppers, and fish float. They added that they see no reason why they cannot do the same thing with a human. The levitation works by using a giant magnetic field, which slightly distorts the orbits of electrons in the frog's atoms.

Little Things Mean a Lot

In Turkey, Mehmet Esirgen, 52, tried to cure his sexual impotence by having a penis transplant—using a donkey as the donor. The wire service Agence France-Presse reported that three times Esirgen brought home a donkey, amputated its sexual organs, and appealed in vain for a doctor to perform the operation. Apparently the third time so annoyed his family that his son shot him in the leg. Esirgen announced that as soon as he recovered from the shooting, he intended to buy a fourth donkey and try again.

Climbing the Family Tree

Childless couples in a remote jungle region of Borneo began stealing orangutan babies from a nature park to raise as their own. Edwin Bosi, who runs the Sepilok rehabilitation center for orangutans, said three or four of the apes disappear every month, adding that some of the animals have turned up in the nearby homes of plantation workers, who shave the animals' body hair and powder their skin to make them look more human.

Side Effect

South Africa's largest game park was forced to end a seven-month program using hormone implants to keep elephants from getting pregnant because the implants kept the elephants in a continuous state of heat. "The bulls were following them around all the time, hassling them," park veterinarian Douw Grobler said, adding that although none of the elephants got pregnant, "this was not the kind of behavior we were looking for."

Getting Them into It Is the Easy Part

Authorities in St. Croiz County, Minnesota, charged two men with rustling after they were caught stuffing six-hundred-pound cows into the back of their Chevrolet Chevette.

Jumbo Sex

Kim Lee Chong, 61, was sentenced to 15 years in jail for trying to have sex with an elephant. After he was caught naked from the waist down standing on a box behind the animal, he insisted the elephant was the reincarnation of his wife, who had died 28 years earlier. "I recognized her immediately by the naughty glint in her eyes," Kim told the court in Phuket, Thailand.

When Turtles Are Outlawed, Only Outlaws Will Have Turtles

Pizza deliverer Troy Brewster was robbed in Balch Springs, Texas, by two men brandishing a snapping turtle. "That sucker was going to bite me. They put him right in my face," said Brewster, who quickly handed over his money pouch with about $50.

Island of Doctor Moreau

• Scientists at Stanford University researching the role of vision in how animals learn where a sound comes from sutured tiny eyeglasses onto the heads of three baby barn owls just as their eyes were beginning to open. The glasses made objects directly in front of the owls appear to be 20 degrees off to the left. The researchers found that the three owls calibrated their hearing to match it with their distorted vision.

• University of Wisconsin researcher Tom Yuill began collaborating with African scientists to see if a species of giant rat considered a delicacy there could be raised in captivity for food. The rat can grow to three or four pounds.

Disappearing Act

Animal trainer Arlan Seidon spent five years as a fugitive before he was arrested in Jefferson, Texas. He managed to elude authorities despite having to conceal two full-grown elephants who were with him the whole time. What's more, he had to secretly acquire 600 pounds of food a day and dispose of 500 pounds of droppings. The 60-year-old man and the elephants—which he raised, then sold, then kidnapped to rescue from abuse, then defied a court order to return them to their owner in New Jersey—spent their first four years moving around the northern United States and Canada before fleeing to Texas. Seidon trucked the elephants to Florida each winter, traveling when weigh scales weren't open and on back roads. He also wore disguises and used a pseudonym.

It's a Living

The Los Angeles *Daily News* reported that Rick Perry, owner of the Van Nuys Rodent Ranch, breeds 200,000 mice and 70,000 rats a year at his industrial park warehouse off the San Diego Freeway. He earns $20,000 to $30,000 a year selling the rodents to local pet stores, which resell them as pets or reptile food. "You don't get rich doing this, but you can get by," said Perry, who got into the business after his wife bought him 16 rats at a garage sale five years ago as a present. "It used to be very relaxing work, but as you grow it becomes more stressful when you have to churn out 10,000 rodents a week."

Baa on Peace

A collapse of sheep prices in Australia in the early 1990s—as low as five cents a head—was blamed on global demilitarization. The London *Sunday Correspondent* observed that Australia had been supplying up to 70 percent of the world's wool, lots of which was used to make army uniforms, the demand for which had plummeted. The paper also suggested that global warming had lowered the need for warm wool clothing.

Just Wear Body Nets

After heavy spring rains and record floods in northern Texas brought predictions of hordes of mosquitoes, members of the Ponderosa Ranch nudist colony near Wills Point hastily built birdhouses to attract purple martins, which feast on the insects.

Escargots, Went

Person or persons unknown stole 153,000 snails from a farm in Hebburn, England, that sells the mollusks to restaurants. Police said they suspected animal rights activists.

Sex Is Its Own Punishment

Israel Zinhanga, 28, told a Zimbabwe court that he had an improper relationship with a cow, but only because he was afraid a human partner might give him AIDS. Agence France-Press reported that after the court sentenced Zinhanga to nine months, he professed his love for the cow and vowed to remain faithful to her during his sentence.

Form a Line

Six people drowned trying to rescue a chicken that fell down a 60-foot well in the Egyptian village of Nazlat Imara. Police said 18-year-old farmer Allam Sabet al-Sayyed, his sister Zeinab, brothers Sayyed and Ahmad, and two elderly farmers who came to help climbed down, one after the other. They all drowned, apparently after being pulled down in the water by an undercurrent. The chicken survived.

Grave-y Train

The corpses of 828 beagles that were among 3,700 irradiated in experiments were removed from the University of California at Davis and buried in the Hanford, Washington, Nuclear Reservation, at a cost of $22 million. The university made $65 million from the cold war research aimed at seeing how long the dogs could live after eating radioactive food. Some lived as long as 18 years.

Cathouse

An official with the Passaic Housing Authority in New Jersey spent $14,800 in federal funds buying cat food and other supplies for some 40 stray cats that he kept in an air-conditioned room at a federally subsidized housing project. A congressional report noted that at first the official claimed the cats were unpaid PHA employees working to catch rats, then changed his story and announced he was running an adoption clearinghouse for cats.

Strange Cargo

• Airport officials in Birmingham, England, wouldn't let Ingrid Hannoway, 32, board her flight to Northern Ireland with her pet tarantula, so she put the animal in an envelope and mailed it to her Belfast address. After postal workers rescued the spider from the mailbox, the Royal Society for the Prevention of Cruelty to Animals announced it would prosecute her, charging, "Mrs. Hannoway had no regard for this spider's welfare whatsoever."

• A Nigerian man stopping at Rome's Fiumicino airport en route from Lagos to Istanbul was arrested when authorities searched his luggage and found 40 parrots. The birds had apparently been drugged before being tied together by their beaks and packed in a suitcase.

• U.S. Customs Service agents at Eagle Pass, Texas, inspected a pickup truck entering from Mexico and found six live snakes in a tool compartment. When they searched the two men in the truck, they found eight more live snakes, each wrapped in socks and pantyhose, hidden in the men's underwear. "In the past, we have found marijuana cigarettes and other drugs," officer Humberto Rodriguez said, "but never snakes in Jockey shorts."

• When police searched a car that they stopped after spotting it weaving on U.S. 19 outside Chiefland, Florida, they found boxes and bags containing 48 rattlesnakes, a Gila monster, 45 nonpoisonous snakes, 67 scorpions, several tarantulas, some lizards, and a parrot. They charged driver, R. Kevin Temple, 35, with illegal possession of wildlife and venomous reptiles.

• Police in Omaha, Nebraska, found 98 young alligators in a man's bedroom. Lieutenant Tom Quinn of the Florida Game and Fresh Water Fish Commission said the man apparently was taking care of the reptiles for a friend after a deal to ship them from Florida to Japan fell through.

• When a Customs agent in Miami searched the luggage of Manuel Frade, 20, an arrival from Venezuela, she touched a pair of jeans and felt something wriggling. It turned out to be 14 juvenile boa constrictors. A further search of Frade's bags found hundreds of tarantulas, their eggs, and 300 poison-arrow frogs, all smuggled in violation of the Endangered Species Act.

• Authorities at Baltimore-Washington International Airport arrested Robert A. Daverio for smuggling after finding more than 250 tortoises and turtles hidden in his suitcase. The reptiles were all less than four inches long.

• Authorities at Spain's Madrid-Barajas airport arrested Francisco Javier Gibert, 29, when a security check found him carrying a live baby crocodile and a baby caiman alligator affixed to small wooden planks inside the lining of his jacket.

Room for One More

Canadian authorities fined George Hyer and Catherine Cornell forty dollars for causing animals distress after the Society for Prevention of Cruelty to Animals raided the couple's mobile home in Drayton Valley, Alberta, and seized 108 cats, 168 pigeons, and 17 doves. Another 100 parakeets were left in the trailer because they were reportedly not in distress. Provincial Judge L. E. Nemirsky also issued a lifetime order limiting Hyer and Cornell to one cat and four birds each.

Lawyers

The Maryland Court of Appeals suspended lawyer Stanley E. Protokowicz Jr. for breaking into the home of a client's estranged wife, putting the family's seven-month-old kitten in the microwave, and zapping it. Protokowicz testified that he indeed put the kitten in the microwave because it was underfoot but turned it on by accident.

Old Habits Die Hard

Residents of Manganeses de las Polvorosa in northern Spain agreed to forgo the custom of throwing a live goat off the church bell tower at their annual festival. Instead, they reassured animal rights groups protesting the event that they would slowly lower the animal from the 65-foot building using a rope. Halfway down, however, the villagers lowering the animal let go of the rope. Villagers below did catch it in a canvas sheet.

Mayor Jose Manuel Gil Barrio defended the ceremony, which began in the nineteenth century after a priest locked a goat in the church belfry during a famine to prevent it from being eaten, but the current priest, Honorino Gonzalez, insisted that goat tossing had no religious significance. "People only do it for fun," he said.

Designer Shedding

Weaver Kim Mikela of Walled Lake, Michigan, reported that an emerging trend is having "a scarf or sweater made from your own dog's hair."

Gimme Shelter

Although the Humane Society of the United States opposes animal testing, the Connecticut Humane Society acknowledged owning $2.7 million worth of stock in firms that do the most animal testing.

Guinea Pigs

Martin Fettman, America's first veterinarian in space, performed the first animal dissections in space aboard the space shuttle *Columbia*. To avoid using anesthesia on the half-dozen white rats so the organs and other removed tissue would be free of chemicals, Fettman used a miniature guillotine to decapitate the animals.

Bozos of the Mist

Ugandan authorities in Kampala reported they were hunting a man who knocks out gorillas with tranquilizer darts, then dresses them in clown outfits.

Too Cuddly for Their Own Good

Robert Jones, 25, admitted pulling a koala bear from a tree on a golf course in Australia, kicking it, stabbing it five times in the neck, hacking off its head, and drinking its blood. When police asked why he did it, Jones said it was hard to explain. After Judge Philip Johnson of the New South Wales District Court ordered Jones released on a three-year good-behavior bond, he said it was "regrettable that the matter proceeded to trial during National Koala Week."

Innocent Weapons

• When a car pulled up beside Clarence Joseph Gland and Kim Denise Williams, who were taking a late-night stroll in Camden, New Jersey, three men got out. One shoved a black snake in Gland's face while the other two took the couple's cash, personal stereo, and a watch.

• Josef Meschede, 44, a farmer from Augsburg, Germany, was charged with murdering his wife by training his bull to attack on command, then luring Karolina Meschede, 40, to his enclosure, hitting her on the head with a pitchfork, and commanding the bull to attack. Police became suspicious when

Meschede tried to cash in more than $300,000 worth of life insurance policies on his wife and contacted dating services before she died.

• Sheriff's deputies in Piru, California, arrested a 13-year-old boy they said assaulted his mother by throwing the family's pet Chihuahua at her. Neither the victim nor the weapon was hurt, according to sheriff's Lieutenant Gary Markley, who observed it was the first Chihuahua assault he had encountered in his 26 years of law enforcement.

Good of the Many Outweighs Needs of the Few

After bringing four tiny frogs from the Seychelles to Japan for an exhibit of exotic wildlife, officials at the Osaka Flower Expo discovered the one-third-inch-long amphibians were almost invisible to the naked eye and tended to hide behind leaves in their displays. Expo officials announced that to enable visitors to see the remarkable creatures, they had decided to kill two of them, preserve them in chemicals, and display them under magnifying glasses. "It was a very sorrowful decision," one official said, "but this is the only way we can show the frogs to as many people as possible."

An outcry by animal lovers persuaded expo officials to concede there was one other way. They said they would show videos of the frogs instead.

Illuminating Solution

British farmers reported success foiling predatory foxes by painting their lambs with phosphorescent spray paint. The product, called Repel, was developed after researchers discovered that lambs glowing in the dark discourages predators. As a further deterrent, the paint is laced with a substance that a Repel spokesperson said "has a taste so horrible that even a hungry fox will never become accustomed to it."

Open Up

Michael Gentner, 23, choked to death after trying to swallow a live, five-inch fish on a dare. Three unidentified friends called 911, but paramedics were unable to resuscitate him, said fire Lieutenant Dennis Ragins, adding, "They could see the tail still sticking out of his mouth."

Fatal Attraction

Veterinarian Ralph Farnsworth of the University of Minnesota recommended that farmers magnetize their cows at the start of the spring tornado season. He explained that the magnets, which are inserted with a pill gun, collect small pieces of metal, which cows often eat while grazing in windblown fields, and "hold them in place so that they cannot move around and injure the animal."

Extinct—But Not Forgotten

• At least six people in Memphis, Tennessee, who paid $2.50 to visit a 1992 zoo exhibit called "Dinosaurs Live!" demanded their money back after discovering that the creatures were computerized, mechanical replicas, not the real thing. "We thought when we opened we would have kids who would be frightened by the dinosaurs," said Ann Ball, a zoo vice president. "But little did I know I would have adults who didn't know dinosaurs were dead."

• Two years later, after 12 fossilized dinosaur eggs went on display at the Memphis Pink Palace Museum, people who saw pictures of the eggs in the newspaper or on television began showing up at the museum claiming to have found their own fossilized eggs. All the eggs turned out to be ordinary round rocks.

Ruffled Feathers

India's social democratic Janata Dal party outraged its opponents in the eastern state of Bihar by capturing parrots and teaching them to recite political slogans at election meetings. The regional Jarkhand Mukti Morcha party demanded that the parrots be released, claiming Dal activists had clipped their wings to prevent them from escaping and starved them to force them to learn the slogans.

Second-Amendment Follies

• Marilyn Anderson, 47, was trying to stop her 10 dogs from fighting when she shot herself, according to Denver police. She explained she routinely fired gunshots into the ceiling to stop the fighting, and said the noise usually worked, but this time it didn't. When she went to clear the weapon, she forgot that she had put a bullet in the gun and shot herself in the hand.

• Robert Tate, 90, tried to shoot at a large rat he thought was hiding under the bed but accidentally shot himself in the hand. Pennsylvania state police in Greene County said Tate awoke from a nightmare he was having about a large rat and believed the rat was under his bed making noises. He reached for a .22-caliber revolver beneath his mattress, and it accidentally fired.

A Cut Above

A Missouri company began marketing plastic replacement testicles for neutered dogs. The jelly bean–shaped Neuticles came in five sizes, ranging in price from $28 for an extra-small pair to $32 for large and are implanted into the scrotum in a two-minute procedure immediately after the natural testicles are removed. "The dog looks the same. He feels the same," inventor Gregg Miller of Buckner, Missouri, insisted. "He doesn't even know he's been neutered."

Love's an Illusion

Officials of Florida Wildlife Park announced they were setting up mirrors around six flamingos, explaining that the birds are more sexually excitable if they're in a group.

Man's Really Best Friend

Authorities in Laurel County, Kentucky, charged Jimmy Earl Humfleet, 33, with killing his uncle after he discovered the uncle having sex with a pit bull. The shooting was recorded on an audiotape of incoming 911 calls, according to former deputy Derek House. In Humfleet's first call, "He stated his uncle was having sexual intercourse with a dog, and he wanted somebody out there, now," House testified at a preliminary hearing. When a 911 dispatcher called back a few minutes later for directions, Humfleet said nothing was wrong. He called back later to report his uncle was molesting a dog. The dispatcher heard arguing and a single gunshot. House testified that when Humfleet returned to the phone, he said, "I shot him."

Caught Necking

The Society of Victor Invictus was formed to honor the memory of Victor the giraffe, who died at England's Maxwell Park Zoo in 1977 after he slipped while mating and was unable to regain his footing. By its tenth year, the society, whose name in Latin means "Victor Unconquered," claimed to have 950 members worldwide.

Real Virtuality

Vietnamese schoolchildren rejected the popular Japanese virtual pets, known as Tamagotchi, in favor of the real thing. A Ho Chi Minh City newspaper reported children buy tiny newly hatched birds, which cost 25 cents each instead of $30 for the electronic alternative. Like the handheld Japanese computer game, the real pets grow and tweet when they need attention or food, die if neglected, and disrupt school classes.

Cloning's Next Challenge

An Australian pet craze is giant cockroaches, which children enjoy picking up and cuddling. Noting the three-inch insects weigh 30 times more than common roaches, Queensland Museum insect curator Geoff Monteith, who discovered them, described them as very robust. He insisted, however, that they eat only dead leaves.

When Guns Are Outlawed

Two police officers in Oxnard, California, reported that while on patrol they encountered a man who came at them wielding a live opossum, "its teeth gnashing alarmingly." The officers apprehended the man after a struggle, during which "the opossum broke free and disappeared into the night."

There'll Always Be an England

Ivan Pope, 29, of Chichester, England, was convicted of frightening a chicken before strangling and crushing it, despite the argument by his lawyer, Terry Brooks, that the chicken didn't have the intellectual capacity to foresee its fate and thus could not have been terrified.

A Stud's Life Isn't What It Used to Be

• In an investigation of the bull semen business, Canadian Press reported that stud bulls "are fixed with plastic vaginas and taught to mount beef steers [castrated males], which are used instead of dairy cows because they can better withstand constant mounting."

• Jackie Sherrill, the football coach of Mississippi State University, arranged to have a bull castrated in front of the team before a game with the University of Texas, whose mascot is a longhorn steer. After the Animal Rescue League filed a complaint, Sherrill defended the demonstration by saying it served two purposes. "One is educational," he explained, noting none of his players knew what a steer was. The other was motivating his team. Asked how a bull's castration would motivate his players, he said, "That's everybody's different perception."

Bird Brains

• Mark Leach, 43, admitted kicking down his neighbor's fence in Oxford, England, and strangling the man's parrot. Leach, who was fined $1,015 and ordered to pay $590 in court costs, said that after four years the bird's loud, incessant squawking finally proved too much.

• An alderman in charge of environmental affairs in Aalsmeer, Netherlands, resigned after confessing that he shot a protected great blue heron in his backyard. Piet Boom said that he lost control after the heron repeatedly gobbled ornamental carp from his garden pond.

• Dallas police reported that someone stole 25 homing pigeons from Dennis Donald Smith. "This doesn't make any sense," said the owner of the trained birds. "The first chance they get, those birds are going to come straight back here."

Osculatory Update

Overfishing of Newfoundland's codfish ended a 40-year-old colorful greeting at one inn in Olde: cod kissing. The custom, adopted by the Quidi Vidi Inn, involves swallowing a shot of Newfoundland screech, a type of cheap rum, then kissing a codfish. "It's about belonging, about being adopted by the people of Newfoundland, and it's a barrel of fun," said innkeeper Linda Hennebury. "We used to use the codfish, but they got smaller and smaller until they were no more, so now we use a turr, a seabird about the size of your hand."

Mutants

• The Department of Energy's Oak Ridge National Laboratory in Tennessee issued a warning that radioactive frogs may be on the loose. At least 100 of the brownish green leopard frogs up to two inches long were caught hopping away from a contaminated pond where they hatched. The frogs were discovered after workers at the facility reported radioactive tires on their vehicles, apparently from running over the creatures, who became contaminated growing up in the mud of a holding basin for waste waters from the lab's nuclear research in the 1940s and 1950s.

• Officials announced that after two months of searching they had been unable to track down a radioactive goat that escaped from the Jornado Experimental Range area in southern New Mexico during an experiment. The animal, dubbed "The Atomic Goat," was one of 62 Angora goats fitted with radioactive isotopes to track their movements. Bob Jenks of the New Mexico Game and Fish Department said his agency was concerned that the isotopes "may be consumed by various species or organisms or transferred along the food chain."

• Scientists studying wildlife in contaminated areas around Chernobyl reported that voles are among the species thriving on radioactive pollution. "These are the most contaminated animals I've seen anywhere," Ron Chesser of the University of Georgia said, observing that although a species of the rodent is mutating at an "incredible rate," it is breeding healthily and producing ever-stronger offspring.

M-I-C-K-E-Y

Scientists finally figured out how to grow humanlike ears on mice. Linda Griffith-Cima, an assistant professor of chemical engineering at Massachusetts Institute of Technology, created an ear-shaped scaffolding of porous, biodegradable fabric. Next, she and University of Massachusetts anesthesiologist Dr. Charles Vacanti distributed human cartilage cells throughout the form, then implanted the prototype ear on the back of a hairless mouse, which nourished the ear until the cartilage cells grew to replace the fiber. Once the technology is perfected, the scientists explained, ears can be transplanted from mice to people who lose theirs in accidents. They said the technique will work for noses, too.

Once Is Enough

When Jason Smallwood, 26, showed up at an indoor rodeo in Bedford County, Virginia, asking to ride a wild bull, he admitted he had never ridden one before. But, he pointed out, he had practiced on a bucking-barrel mechanical ride. He lasted about three seconds before the bull threw him, then trampled him and tossed him against a fence, killing him. "He said he wanted to try it once," Todd Wood, a friend, noted. "He always wanted to try something once."

Chinese Chickens

Poultry scientists in Taiwan reported success using acupuncture to prevent broodiness in hens, a condition in which the hen sits on her egg to hatch it instead of laying more eggs. The treatment involves inserting a needle into the hen's head between the nostrils on the beak and leaving it there for two days.

Sorry about That

A pepper spray that is popular with hikers in Alaska for protection against bears actually attracts the animals, according to U.S. Geological Survey researcher Tom Smith. While observing brown bear activity, he noticed a bear rolling on a rope that had been sprayed with the red pepper extract. To test the link, Smith said he sprayed the extract on the beach. Several bears approached and began rolling in it like "a 500-pound cat with a ball of catnip," Smith said. "Little did we know this stuff was like mayonnaise on bologna."

The maker of the pepper spray, Counterassault, reacted to Smith's findings by changing its package description from bear repellent to bear deterrent. General manager Pride Johnson explained the product still does its job because it's designed to be sprayed into an attacking bear's face, not worn like mosquito spray. Even so, he noted, "We've had some parents spray it on their children because it says 'bear repellent.' "

Mouth-to-Beak

Daniel Burnson, 12, was explaining his chicken-cleaning technique to judges at the Western Washington State Fair when his prize hen passed out and fell into a bowl of soapy water. Witnesses said judge Sherry Milligan grabbed the limp bird, opened its beak, and breathed into it to resuscitate it.

Quiet, Please

Police in Hicksville, New York, arrested Ruben Caro, 32, for trying to shoplift two lovebirds from a pet store by stuffing the $90 birds down his jeans. Store employees were alerted when they heard the pants chirping.

Capital Idea

Manila judge Maximiano Asuncion recommended that people in the Philippines who are convicted of crimes carrying the death sentence should be made to wrestle poisonous snakes inside a giant tank open to public view.

High Jinks

Cheap poison used by the New York City health department to control rats instead caused them to become "psychotic," according to workers in the Bronx, who complained that the drugged rodents were strolling into offices in broad daylight. Health department spokesperson Sam Friedman denied that the city's extermination efforts were making the rats crazy, but workers also complained that they were finding dead rats in their desk drawers and filing cabinets.

Sunk

Ten penguins died of lead poisoning in just one month at the Henry Doorly Zoo in Omaha, Nebraska. Director Lee Simmons said the gentoo penguins died from eating small lead pellets that fell out of ankle weights used by scuba divers who maintain the penguin's water tanks.

We're from the Government, We're Here to Help

Using a gill net to catch illegally introduced lake trout at Yellowstone National Park backfired, according to federal biologists. The net, which kills the fish it catches, snared only four lake trout compared with 150 cutthroat, the species the biologists are trying to save.

Undersea Coal Miners?

Scientists announced that bottle-nosed dolphins in the Gulf of Mexico have begun developing black lung disease.

It's a Dog's Life

In Wilmington, North Carolina, thieves pushed a female dog through a window at a gas station, distracting the male guard dog inside while they made off with about a hundred old pennies, several rings, and a grinder.

Steady Job

Officials of India's Bombay Municipal Corporation oversee 85 "night rat killers" (technically referred to as NRKs), who patrol the city at night beating rats to death with sticks. Each NRK has a quota of 25 rats a night. Most expert NRKs fill their quota within the first two hours of their shift each night, leaving the rest of their hours free for other work, according to one overseer, who added, "I can easily make out a rat beaten to death from a poisoned rat," for which an NRK receives no credit.

Omnivore's Digest

• Joseph Vera, 29, of Victorville, California, was found guilty of animal cruelty for killing and barbecuing his neighbor's collie–pit bull terrier, Astro. Claiming self-defense, Vera insisted the dog attacked him and that he hadn't eaten in two days. "I stood over him, looking at him. I saw different types of meals I could make out of him." He went on to describe how he seasoned Astro with salt, pepper, and lemon and proceeded to barbecue his ribs on a grill in his front yard. "I didn't have corn tortillas to make tacos, so I took the ribs and barbecued the ribs," Vera told the court. The prosecutor charged that Vera killed the dog in revenge for an earlier argument with his neighbor over a VCR. He also pointed out that after the killing, Vera put Astro's head on his neighbor's front gate.

• Al's Oasis in Oacama, South Dakota, added a Buffalo Burger to its menu, touting it as "100 percent pure buffalo" from the "herd that appeared in *Dances with Wolves*."

• Solo Leibowitz defended plans to export dogs from Israel to the Philippines, where they are considered a delicacy. "Instead of killing stray dogs," he said, "it would be humanitarian to fly them to Asia to feed starving people."

• Bats on Guam and other South Pacific islands face extinction because people there keep eating them. According to a World Wildlife Fund report, the indigenous Chamorros, who make up 45 percent of Guam's population, have been feasting on fruit bats for 2,500 years and consider them a delicacy.

Even though fewer than 500 bats remain on an island with 50,000 Chamorros, they are sold in grocery stores, from roadside stands, and by door-to-door vendors for between $25 and $40 each. Despite laws to protect endangered species, Guam illegally imports about 7,000 frozen bats a year, mostly from the Philippines.

• Swallowing live sardines is the tonic in India, where as many as 150,000 asthma sufferers flock to Hyderabad each spring for the annual handout of "fish medicine." An herbal concoction, reportedly a miracle cure for asthma, is placed in the mouth of a live sardine, which the sufferer then swallows, repeating the treatment at home every 15 days. The philanthropists who have organized the event for more than 100 years claim that 98 percent of the people who follow the treatment for at least three years are cured.

• Cat is now popular at high-class restaurants in Nanjing, according to the *Economic Evening News*. The paper also reported that a merchant there who added fresh cat to his customary specialty of dog meat now sells as many as 50 cats a day, killing and dressing them after the buyer chooses the one he wants.

• Japanese farmers in Kisakata reported success stopping crows from damaging their rice and soybean crops by trapping 200 of the birds a month and eating them. The newspaper *Mainichi* quoted the mayor of the coastal town as saying, "They taste quite good."

Take Off the Blinders

Two racehorses died at Churchill Downs in Louisville, Kentucky, when they collided head-on. The animals were completing a morning workout when Miss Carson's bridle broke. The four-year-old filly threw her exercise rider and headed back up the stretch. "I was going around the turn and here comes the loose horse," said Dean Flatland, who was riding five-year-old gelding Rare Reason. "I was trying to go one way or the other, and the horse just kept coming straight at me—and bang."

Cows and Effect

• University of Illinois researchers reported they were studying how to turn old newspapers into cattle food. According to animal scientist Larry Berger, one cow eats 20 to 25 pounds of roughage a day—enough to consume the 5 million to 6 million tons of old newspaper collected in the United States if 30 percent of the bovine diet is treated newsprint.

• The federal Environmental Protection Agency gave $500,000 to Utah State University to round up rangeland cattle and fit them with special breathing devices to measure how much methane cows release when they burp. Aimed at determining how cow burps contribute to global warming, the project expands a 1991 $300,000 grant to Washington State University to measure methane produced by bovine flatulence. Animal nutritionist Kenneth Olson, head of the Utah State study, said that gas passed at either end of the cow is insignificant, explaining that he believes cows get rid of "over 90 percent" of their methane by exhaling it.

Devaluation

The British Small Animal Veterinary Association announced that each year of a dog's life no longer equals seven human years. Instead, the association recommended multiplying a dog's age by five to determine the human equivalent.

Super Fresh

When raw fish lost its novelty for Japanese gourmets, they turned to eating fish live. "The food moves around a lot—that's the whole idea," said Sunao Uehara, a chef at Chunagon seafood restaurant in Tokyo's Ginza district. Waiters serve the fish—shrimp, flounder, lobster, firefly squid, loaches, sea bream, and eel—wiggling and with their eyes and mouths moving, then quickly slice open the midsection and gut them for patrons.

Coincidences Most Fowl

• A rare American bittern migrating from North America to Central America was blown off course and wound up crossing the Atlantic Ocean. It concluded its flight by alighting on the ground in Wexford in southeastern Ireland, where it was promptly killed and eaten by a hunting dog. "This is a tragedy," ornithologist Killian Mullarney said. "It was the first American bittern known to have reached Ireland since 1973, so a lot of people, including many from Britain, would have liked to have seen it."

• A gray-cheeked thrush, apparently blown off course while migrating from Canada to South America, flew 3,000 miles across the Atlantic to Gloucestershire, England, only to be killed when it flew into a plate-glass door at the visitors center at the headquarters of Britain's Wildfowl and Wetland Trust.

• While bird watchers from across England were gathered at the Leicestershire reservoir to watch the migration of the rare red-necked phalarope, a four-foot-long pike jumped out of the water and devoured the bird in one bite. "It was like a scene from *Jaws*," one bird watcher said. "One second the bird was swimming, the next there was a snap and a splash and it vanished."

Belling the Cat

The best way to tell penguins apart, according to scientists studying the migration routes of the look-alike birds in the Antarctic, is by gluing bar codes, like those used on supermarket packages, to their beaks. John Croxall, a biologist with the British Antarctic Survey, said scanners to read the bar codes could then be placed along regularly traveled penguin paths.

No Sex, Please, We're Pigs

A one-year rise in British pork prices of 9 percent in 1996 was initially attributed to high demand in Japan, but upon further investigation, Britain's Central Statistical Office concluded the real reason was lack of sex. High temperatures the previous summer meant hogs spent more time deep in cool mud instead of breeding. Beef prices were more stable, according to *Guardian* economics writer Larry Elliott, who pointed out that cows are usually artificially inseminated and "do not have the chance to say no."

Part of the Scenery

Contract workers repairing a stretch of roadway in Pennsylvania's Schuylkill County paved over a deer carcass lying about Route 895. State transportation engineer Walter Bortree said the contractor probably just didn't see the animal, but Keith Billig, the mayor of nearby Bowmanstown, pointed out, "The deer was lying there dead for three to four weeks. You can't miss it. It's in a straightaway."

Music Hath Charms

Vietnamese bird poachers began flocking to bird sanctuaries with cassette tape players after discovering that the Brazilian dance tune the "Lambada" puts birds into a trance. The *Saigon Times Daily* commented that "with this sort of hunting, birds in the Mekong Delta are in danger of extinction."

Sore Loser

When airport authorities in Brasilia told departing Iraqi diplomat Kadaru Isamal that he couldn't take two parrots home with him because it is illegal to export wild birds from Brazil, Isamal became so infuriated that he strangled the birds to death on the spot.

What's My Line?

Jamie Buchsbaum, 26, attracted media attention in Cincinnati by trying to earn a living dressing giant dead cockroaches in celebrity costumes. Buchsbaum said he started dressing up roaches in 1988 when he made a Santa roach and eight tiny roach-deer. His Elvis Proachley creation was a South American giant roach dressed in a white jumpsuit and blue suede shoes. Buchsbaum explained most of the roaches he uses died of natural causes at the Cincinnati Zoo's insect exhibit, where he works as a volunteer.

Fatal Attraction

Pilots Richard Halstead and Lawrence Schneider were killed when their small planes collided near Alaska's Denali National Park after they spotted a moose. Witnesses on the ground said both pilots were circling, seemed to be looking at the moose, and apparently failed to notice each other before hitting head-on.

Unreasonable Expectation

Sherman Hill argued in a San Jose, California, court—unsuccessfully—that his dog Queenie should count as a passenger in a designated car-pool lane because it watched for cars and warned its master. Hill noted that his eyesight is failing and explained he was training the dog as a "seeing eye driver."

Mush, Fifi

John Suter of Chugiak, Alaska, entered a team of poodles in the 1,049-mile Iditarod sled race in 1990, despite the insistence by some of his competitors that poodles are not sled dogs. In 1988, the first year he raced poodles, his team finished 38th out of 52. The next year, his poodles had to drop out because their long coats became wet and were in danger of freezing.

Fowl Play

• Australian Roger Schlup filed a lawsuit against veterinarian Ross Perry, seeking $192,000 for ruining his bird's sex life. He charged that when he took the South American macaw to Perry for treatment of a broken right leg, Perry somehow broke the bird's other leg, then failed to fix either one properly. Schlup explained that strong legs are essential for the macaws' intricate mating ritual, which requires "the male and female to stand on a perch next to each other, twist around and align their rear ends." Schlup said that as a result of Perry's negligence, he has no chance of breeding his willing but unable bird and selling its offspring.

• A man accused of having sex with a turkey at the poultry plant where he worked in Adams County, Pennsylvania, admitted assaulting the 20-pound bird in an employee shower but blamed his coworkers for encouraging him. After Timothy Bodkins explained that two coworkers offered him $12 and three cans of chewing tobacco to sodomize the turkey while one of them held it, District Justice John C. Zepp III fined him $750.

Animals on Duty

• After attacks by humans and aircraft failed to end an invasion of locusts in China's Xinjiang province, the government trained an army of 100,000 chickens to try to control the insects, which have infested grasslands, housing complexes, and offices. Xinhua news agency reported the chickens underwent "a special 60-day training program shortly after birth."

The program involves teaching them to recognize and follow a specific color worn by the human supervisor. "We don't have to train them to want to eat locusts," said Yu Xiaoguo, an official working on the project. "They do that naturally."

• Jordanian officials enlisted armies of fish to help battle warm-weather algae that had polluted the water supply of the capital. "Various kinds of fish have been released in the waterways leading to Amman's Zai water treatment plant to eat the algae and other suspended particles before the chemical purification process," Water Minister Hani al-Mulqi told reporters, explaining that this action "solved the pollution problem at its roots."

Wait for the Reruns

Japan's Asahikawa cable television, which serves 12,000 households, began airing the Goldfish Channel as a joke, but its popularity kept it on the air. Around-the-clock, commercial-free broadcasts alternate 12 hours of goldfish with 12 hours of tropical fish.

Mind-Blowing Experience

To try to rid its parking garages of pigeons, whose droppings get all over travelers' cars, Denver International Airport began scattering corn soaked in the drug Avitrol, which officials described as "pigeon LSD." Avitrol is supposed to make the birds forget their whereabouts, but it has made some forget how to fly, according to officials, who reported that about 100 pigeons had crashed and died.

Pecking Order

Pet therapist Darrian Lundy switched from dogs to chickens for her therapeutic sessions at health-care facilities in Riverside County, California, explaining, "It gets people talking who haven't talked all week." She began training the two birds she uses now when they were one week old, bringing them into her home, hand-feeding them, and training them to behave on leashes. Although the birds generally raise patients' spirits, Lundy said they have to be passed around in flat boxes because "unlike other animals, you can't housebreak chickens."

Hostage Situation

Peter Lerat, 33, who had been sought by Toronto police for holding a Canada goose hostage during a robbery, was arrested a month later on charges of threatening a raccoon. Police said Lerat swore he would hit a two-month-old raccoon on the head with a rock if passers-by did not give him $35. After being charged with extortion, Lerat tried to make his first court appearance stark naked. "Apparently he left here with his clothes," police Officer Bruce Kane said, "but he refused to put them on."

Mistaken Identity

Bug zappers fry the wrong bugs, according to University of Delaware entomologist Douglas Tallamy. After collecting 13,789 insects killed by six bug zappers over the course of a summer, Tallamy found that only 31 of them were biting flies. Nearly 2,000 of the dead bugs were potentially beneficial insects and thousands more were harmless species. Tallamy concluded that the bug zapper "is a totally useless device."

Still Clucking

When farmer Janet Bonney found one of her chickens frozen under her porch in Harpswell, Maine, she tried to put the bird's body in a shoe box for burial, but its frozen legs wouldn't bend. She tried dunking the bird in hot water to thaw it enough to make it fit, but then she heard it breathe and used mouth-to-beak resuscitation to revive it.

Roll Me Over in the Clover

Scientists at Australian National University announced the development of an environmentally friendly lawn mower powered by rabbits that cuts grass and fertilizes lawns at the same time. Nigel Wace, inventor of the device, made from bicycle wheels, wire netting, and buckets, explained that the project was delayed because at first the scientists couldn't get the rabbits to move the six-foot cylindrical contraption, dubbed the Rolling Rabbit Run, around a lawn. Then they figured out they should put two males inside. Earlier trials using a male and a female rabbit failed because the animals kept stopping to have sex.

Sacrificial Lambs

Animals at Jerusalem's Biblical Zoo were deprived of their usual food in 1998 when all bread products were removed for Passover. Even though the dietary ban against leavened food products applies to people, not animals, zoo officials said they were concerned that if the animals kept to their normal diets, devout zookeepers and visitors might come in contact with the banned foods.

Another Idea Begging to Run Amok

To rid itself of mosquitoes, the town of Belle Glade, Florida, announced it was importing even bigger, giant Burmese mosquitoes to eat them. The newcomers are 15 times bigger than normal mosquitoes, and their larvae eat the larvae of native mosquitoes, according to entomologist Eric Schreiber, head of the experiment. He reassured residents that they have nothing to fear from adult Burmese mosquitoes, which he insisted feed on nectar, not human blood.

Pussy-Whipped

Police in Tempe, Arizona, arrested Edward Lee Treaster, 21, for hitting his roommate in the face with a cat. The force of the blow injured David Little and killed the cat.

Eager to Experiment

Marin County, California, delayed construction of a proposed $30-million animal research center until it could complete a telephone survey costing $4,500 to determine how the center would affect county residents' self-esteem. The center's administrative director, Mary McEacheron, blamed the need for the survey on "rodent activists."

Full-Body Cast

After a passing auto crushed the spine of a rare female rock python in a remote region of South Africa, a medical team in Pietersburg performed a pioneering three-hour operation to reset the vertebrae by drilling holes and securing the bone to special pins with surgical wire.

Nonmultiplying Rabbits

The navy announced it would spend $60,000 to find out why a species of marsh rabbit is disappearing on Cudjoe and Summerland islands in the Florida Keys. The rabbit is named for *Playboy* magazine founder Hugh Hefner. When Hefner heard that anyone wishing to donate money to research the endangered animal's disappearance could name the animal, he pledged the funds, and the rabbit was dubbed *Palustris hefneri*. A controversy ensued over the propriety of *Playboy* funding such a venture, however, and Hefner never delivered the money. The navy, which owns 5,000 acres on the islands and wants to develop more, then decided it would fund the project, although it wouldn't rename the rabbit.

Misdirection

Norwegian scientists tracking the migratory routes of wild salmon were excited to pick up a radio signal from one fish they had given up for lost. They followed the signal to the city of Stavanger, where they found the fish—in a fisherman's freezer.

Driven to Distraction

Wendy Maines was driving through Versailles, New York, when she saw five dogs attacking a cat. She stopped to rescue the cat, scaring off the dogs by honking her horn and slamming the door. Figuring the cat had run into the woods, she started to drive off but felt a bump. It was the cat, now flat. "Maybe," she said afterward, "it was just Mother Nature's way of telling me to mind my own business."

Desperate Measures

When sanitation workers in Uniondale, New York, arrived at the home of Roderick Baker, 70, to clean up his garbage-filled yard, he tried to keep them from removing the 20 tons of debris by holding 140 chickens hostage at knifepoint. After threatening to kill one chicken a minute until the sanitation crew left his property, he killed three of the birds before authorities intervened. "We showed up, and the guy went a little bit psycho, took out a large knife, and started cutting off the heads of chickens," said Larry Wallach, special investigator for the Nassau County Society for the Prevention of Cruelty to Animals. "We told him to stop, then the sergeant came over and arrested him."

Little Things Mean a Lot

Protesting policies by the governments of Norway and Canada that encourage selling seal penises to Asia, where they are considered aphrodisiacs, the International Fund for Animal Welfare placed an ad in British periodicals that featured a photo of John Wayne Bobbitt's detached private part. The copy read: "When it happened to John Wayne Bobbitt, it got worldwide exposure. When it happens to 10,000 seals, it gets slightly less coverage."

The Profit Motive

Scientists announced that dairy animals can be genetically engineered to secrete certain medical drugs in their milk. Writing in the journal *Biotechnology*, the researchers said altered livestock would be commercially valuable as "living factories" by producing certain types of drugs that are now very difficult or expensive to manufacture.

Good Sports

Hawaiian lawmakers approved a bill to legalize cockfighting. The measure provides that instead of being outfitted with the traditional leg spurs, the roosters must wear tiny padded gloves on their feet.

Collared

• Police investigating a convenience store holdup in Portland, Oregon, had little trouble locating suspect Clarence Craig Anderson, 39. They said he had been in such a hurry to make his getaway that he left his dog behind, tied up outside the store. Police looked at the dog's tags and found Anderson's name and address.

• In West Palm Beach, Florida, one of the prosecution witnesses against Rodney Thomas was the police dog whom Thomas was charged with trying to strangle when police tried to arrest him for burglary. Circuit Court Judge Peter Blanc let the dog take the witness stand to show the jury how loud it barked to warn Thomas to surrender.

Just Be Glad It Wasn't Cows

Although rats are revered in Hindu mythology as the steed of the elephant god Ganesh, Air India announced it was shrugging off religious qualms and eradicating rats aboard its aircraft after flights to Tokyo, New York, and London were delayed in the same month by rat infestation.

Old Ways Work

Seeking a cheaper way to kill stray dogs than shooting them with shotguns, the town council in Kuantan, Malaysia, hired aborigines to train its staff in the use of blowpipes. The *New Straits Times* reported the staff will use the blowpipes to stun the dogs with tranquilizers, then hand them over to the town's Veterinary Services Department to kill with lethal injections.

There's Gratitude for You

Authorities on South Africa's Marion Island killed all the wild cats on the island, 46 years after the cats were introduced to stem a plague of mice. The Environmental Ministry said the animals were ignoring the mice and preying on the territory's birds.

Shotgun Approach

South Africa announced it would shoot all pigeons in its northwest diamond-producing area because the birds are being used to smuggle gems out of the country. "Diamonds are leaving the country in a manner which is extremely worrying," said Manda Msomi, the chair of Parliament's public enterprises committee. "Diamonds are being strapped onto the body of pigeons and flown out of the country. The law now is to shoot all pigeons on sight."

Love's a Bitch

Authorities charged Frederick Daniel Presley of Piscataway, New Jersey, with raping at least 20 large female dogs adopted from area animal shelters over the past seven years.

Of Mice and Men

Johns Hopkins University researchers announced they had succeeded in turning docile mice into sexually aggressive killers by altering their brain chemistry. Dr. Solomon Snyder, one of the scientists, couldn't say whether the same imbalance might explain violent criminal behavior, but he did point out that he is impressed how often "mouse behavior can predict human behavior."

Why They Call It Dope

Authorities in southern India reported that drug addicts there are paying to be bitten on the tongue by snakes. Drug therapist Prakhas Chandran, a worker at a therapy center in Paloarivattom, warned that a bite from the unidentified snake could be deadly, but he noted that the venom is strong enough to give a bitten addict a high lasting up to 16 hours.

Political Hazards

A chameleon being used in a political commercial for Canada's Socred party died after filming. Peter Hamilton, director of the animal rights group Lifeforce, said the lizard was worked to death and treated callously during the eighthour shoot. Jess Ketchum, Socred director of operations, said the chameleon's death was unrelated to the commercial, noting, "We were told that the animal had some sort of health problem."

Literal Misinterpretation

A troupe of British acrobats had to miss its opening performance at the Knoxville, Tennessee, World Festival after U.S. Customs officials put its animal costumes in quarantine. The officials feared the boxes of costumes—marked RABBIT EARS, CAT PAWS and GIRAFFE—contained whole animals or parts of them. (The GIRAFFE actually had nothing to do with animals—it's a circus term for a six-foot unicycle.)

Decorating Nature

• Bettie Phillips of Hiddenite, North Carolina, was charged with animal cruelty after she pierced the ears of a fawn and put earrings on it. Phillips told police that she found the fawn abandoned along the roadside and took it home to care for it until it was old enough to be released into the wild. She said that she pierced its ears because she "thought it would be pretty."

• Cattle on the Malaysian resort island of Pulau Langkawi had their ears pierced and fitted with red plastic reflectors to prevent road accidents at night. Officials explained that mechanization in rice fields left many of the island's cattle unemployed and untended. What's more, accident reports suggested the cattle apparently like sitting on the roads at night. Ismail Abu of the Automobile Association said the reflectors are a good idea but only a start, noting, "That takes care of the front of the cow. But what about the back?"

More Than Mere Ornamentation

Scientists said the key to saving the wading birds of Florida's giant Everglades ecosystem might turn out to be the plastic pink flamingos that dot suburban lawns throughout the state. Teams from the South Florida Water Management District began installing the familiar wire-legged creatures, newly painted white, in ponds in a northern section of the threatened swamp, hoping the lawn ornaments will lure their feathered counterparts to the ponds.

Moozak

• Cows like music, according to researcher Alicia Evans. Presenting her findings at the annual meeting of the Indiana Academy of Science in New Albany, Indiana, she said that classical music caused one herd to give 5.5 percent more milk. When Evans switched to Kiss, milk production fell 6 percent. Country music brought a similar drop. When she used another herd, however, the cows disliked classical and chamber music and loved Kiss. "The cows are saying not so much that they like hard rock or classical," Evans concluded. "They're saying they don't like silence."

• Suffolk, Virginia, high school student David Merrell finished first in regional and state science fairs by demonstrating the effects of music on lab mice. After the mice ran through a maze in about 10 minutes, Merrell played classical music to one group and heavy metal to another for 10 hours a day. After three weeks, the mice exposed to classical music made it through the maze in a minute and a half. The rock music group took 30 minutes. Merrell added he "had to cut my project short because all the hard-rock mice killed each other. None of the classical mice did that."

Get It Right

The August 9, 1996, *Pittsburgh Post-Gazette* published the following correction: "A photo caption in Wednesday's editions about a newborn gorilla at the Pittsburgh Zoo incorrectly identified a male gorilla in the picture. It was the brother of the infant, not the father."

Taxes at Work

The U.S. government acknowledged that its military satellites are used to monitor dung heaps in the Australian outback. The satellite reports help Australian researchers track the droppings of cattle, sheep, kangaroos, and goats to determine whether overgrazing in the sparse land is caused by farmers or nature.

In the Mood for Love

• When Daiko, a female gorilla at Japan's Hamamatsu City Zoo, failed to get pregnant because she and her mate didn't have sex often enough, her keepers started showing Daiko videotapes of wild gorillas mating, hoping to arouse her. "The problem is that there aren't that many videos showing gorillas having sex," veterinarian Rikio Nakazawa explained. "If there were a porno video of gorillas, we'd really like to get our hands on it."

• In Harfsen, Netherlands, a 2,640-pound bull named Sunny Boy produced his millionth dose of semen, a feat widely believed to be unequaled in cattle breeding, according to Ronald van Giessen, head of the KI Oost cattle-breeding cooperative. Van Giessen said the seven-year-old bull could be the father of as many as 600,000 calves.

Roadkill Rage

Two years after being kicked in the head by a horse, Melyn Richman, 46, of Skaneateles, New York, painted a sign outside her home calling the horse's owner, neighbor George Wolff, a "sleazy lawyer." When Wolff tried to remove the sign, Richman reportedly rubbed the wet paintbrush in his face, then pulled a .38-caliber pistol and threatened him. According to a sheriff's department report, Richman said that Wolff threw her down in the road next to a dead raccoon, which she picked up and hurled at him. "The dead raccoon was my only means of self-defense," Richman said. "I had no choice."

Catsicles

State police shot and killed Rolf Rahn when he emerged from his home in Genoa, New York, after a 16-hour standoff that began when he shot a plumber who was working on his well. During the standoff, Rahn announced to police that he was an alien of superior intelligence who was waiting for a spaceship. After the siege, police found the remains of 49 cats and one rabbit in Rahn's freezer, all neatly stacked and labeled in freezer bags. "The thing that struck me was how neat it all was," Animal Control Officer Marty Milliman said, noting that the labels not only gave the date of death and time of freezing, but also showed that several of the cats and kittens had been cooked in the oven or heated on heating pads to make them "pliable" enough for freezing. Two labels said demons killed the cats. One said Rahn injected the cat with rubbing alcohol because it was "lying on the floor too much."

Remember to Change the Litter Box

The Third District Court of Appeals ruled that John M. Butler could keep two four-foot alligators as pets in his suburban Miami home. The ruling came two years after he applied for a state permit but was turned down, according to court records, when investigators showed up at his mobile home and "found both alligators in the respondent's bed" and Butler bleeding from gator bites.

What's in a Name?

• Tanzanian magistrate Onesmo Zunda ordered that a pregnant dog named Immigration be executed because the name offended a "highly respected and law-abiding government department." After the dog had been beaten to death,

Chief Justice Francis Nyalali reviewed the case and called Zunda's ruling "stupid."

• In Tampa, Florida, Circuit Court Judge Daniel Gallagher ordered a three-year-old German shepherd named Hitler to be put to death for biting three people. The judge noted, "One person said, 'With a name like that, he's got to be bad.' "

There Go the Donkeys and Elephants

India's chief election commissioner, T. N. Seshan, barred political candidates and their parties from using animals as symbols. He explained that the official action was necessary to stop supporters of rival factions from torturing and killing the actual animals representing their opponents.

Bugsy

• Japan's Ministry of International Trade and Industry reacted to an international trade ban on tortoiseshells by announcing that it was spending $4 million to study the feasibility of a government-funded program to breed cockroaches. The insects would save the jobs of 1,500 craftsmen, who had been using the tortoiseshells to fashion combs, jewelry, and frames for eyeglasses, by providing them a new material.

• In China's Jiangxi province, Yang Siqi, a former exterminator suffering from snail fever, gastritis, and a neurotic disorder, cured himself after orthodox treatment failed by eating large quantities of termites for three months. Believing afterward that termites have a "magical medical power," he turned his interests to medicine and, according to New China News Agency, opened three factories that make termite-based drugs to treat a variety of ills.

Buyer Beware

After paying $19,000 for a German shepherd, actor John Candy filed suit against the man who sold him the dog. He pointed out he took the action after learning that the going price for a dog with its pedigree is only $1,500 to $4,500.

Eureka

Gay Balfour of Cortez, Colorado, started a business to remove pesky prairie dogs from urban areas or on farms by using a powerful vacuum system. The prairie dogs are sucked from their burrows up a tube four inches in diameter and 50 feet long, then slide along a padded deflector plate, and are dumped into a tank in his truck alive "but somewhat confused," Balfour said, revealing that the idea for the business came to him in a dream.

How Soon Before They Get Their Own Talk Show?

• U.S. Department of Agriculture inspectors advised Carmen Shaw, who cares for sick and orphaned animals at her Back to Nature Wildlife Refuge in Bithlo, Florida, to get Judy, a 32-year-old five-pound capuchin monkey, a television set or a VCR to "enrich her environment."

• Derek Allen, a farmer in Rampisham, England, reported that the tin roof of his pigsty acts as a radio receiver, picking up signals from a nearby British Broadcasting Corporation transmitter. Allen said the broadcasts in 36 languages and news bulletins "seem to soothe" the pigs, adding, "I'm sure my pigs know more about what's going on than I do."

• Apple Computers appointed Koko, the gorilla who uses sign language, to the advisory board of a program studying the nature of intelligence. To allow Koko to take part in meetings, the company created a special computer to give her an audible voice.

More Koko Feats

• When Koko turned 25 in 1996, she used sign language to ask the researchers at the Gorilla Foundation in Woodside, California, for a box of "scary" rubber snakes and lizards.

• Primatologist Robert Sapolsky discovered that Koko likes to gossip. "After watching one of her human teachers argue with his girlfriend," he reported, "Koko couldn't help telling another human teacher about it."

• When Koko declared that she wanted to have a baby, zoo officials allowed her to view pictures and videos of prospective mates. She chose a 10-year-old gorilla from the Cincinnati Zoo named Ndume, pointing to Ndume's video and asking for it to be replayed while ignoring videos of other possible mates. Ndume was then flown to the Gorilla Foundation.

Gender Benders

• Human waste dumped into the environment can cause sex changes in wildlife, according to Dutch researchers at the TNO-Nutrition and Food Research Institute in Delft. After they exposed carp to a chemical found in sewage, the sex organs atrophied in the males and some developed an oviduct, which female fish use to lay eggs. Researcher Sylvia Gimeo said the chemical is responsible for feminizing animals, including fish and alligators, and other researchers suspect the same effect could be causing declining fertility among human males being reported in some European cities.

• Male roaches, Britain's most common freshwater fish, are turning into females on account of pollution and human waste, according to a study by Brunel University. Researchers discovered that 100 percent of the male roaches in the Nene and Aire Rivers were taking on female characteristics, in extreme cases losing their testes and developing ovarian tissue.

Leash Lease

• Although having dogs as pets is banned in Beijing as an offensive luxury, citizens who go to Friends of the Dog Park can rent them to play with. The cost for 10 minutes is about 23 cents.

• Masahiro Kobayashi's Tokyo pet shop, Perro Moco,

began offering customers a rent-a-pet service. The business originally rented animals to television and film crews, but Kobayashi decided that the animals were not getting enough human interaction, so he began offering them to people who for some reason can't have a pet of their own. A four-hour walk with a cat or a small dog costs $25, while larger dogs cost $40.

Forgotten Veterans

• After East Germany finally knocked down the Berlin Wall in 1989, officials ordered the deaths of as many as 10,000 attack-trained German shepherds because they were too dangerous to retrain or offer up for adoption as pets. Breaching the wall also released thousands of rabbits who had flourished in the enclosed strips of no-man's land.

• Dolphins became a casualty of the end of the cold war, as dozens trained by the former Soviet Union for military use were sold to traveling shows and circuses in Europe and the Far East for up to $60,000 each. Starting in 1956, the Soviets captured hundreds of dolphins from the Black Sea and trained them to plant mines, find stray missiles, and attack enemy divers, but the animals are no longer affordable under current military budgets. "These dolphins have been horribly abused during their training," World Society for the Protection of Animals expert Richard O'Barry told *The European* in 1994. "Now they are being discarded and sold off to end their lives in disgusting concrete pools. This is not just a local problem, it is a disease. Russian dolphins are turning up everywhere."

• The U.S. Navy announced that it, too, was cutting its elite squad of 100 trained dolphins—who guard anchored ships and hunted mines in Vietnam and the Persian Gulf—by sending 25 to amusement centers, aquariums, or parks. The navy will keep the remaining dolphins, along with 25 sea lions and beluga whales, at a cost of $15,000 to $20,000 a year to feed and maintain each one.

• The Swiss Army discharged 30,000 carrier pigeons from its ranks after 77 years of using pigeons to deliver spy-proof messages. Explaining the move was part of updating its communications system, the army said it planned to retrain 12 of the birds to race on the European pigeon circuit.

Statues' Revenge

Police in Iran's holy city of Qom began a crackdown on pigeon rearing and racing—popular hobbies regarded by authorities as pastimes of idlers—by beheading 12,000 birds in one month.

Government-Think

In an effort to increase the supply of nutrients in the water for the growth of younger salmon, Oregon's Department of Fish and Wildlife started stocking 26 coastal streams with dead salmon.

Love Hurts

Babu, a 14-year-old Indian elephant at China's Zhengzhou city zoo, was engaging in amorous play with a female across a fence, according to the Xinhua news agency, when his trunk got caught and a large part was severed. Limb specialists summoned from across the country spent 17 hours reattaching the trunk.

User's Fees

Under pressure to show a profit, China's Siberian Tiger Park in the northeast province of Heilongjiang began relying on tourists to feed the animals. Visitors buy live chickens ($5) or pheasants ($12) to feed to the endangered tigers, then watch the hunt. Since the tigers soon tire of the game, zoo officials encourage tourists to try something more substantial, offering live cows for $190.

Say Cheese

Maricopa County, Arizona, Sheriff Joe Arpaio proposed equipping four German shepherds with miniature video cameras to keep tabs on 800 prisoners at his "tent-city" jail. Arpaio said the camera equipment would cost $10,000.

Snakes Alive

Indonesian military authorities announced plans to deploy at least 20 pythons to help safeguard polling places in central Java during general elections by scaring off antigovernment demonstrators. Lieutenant Colonel Harry Purdianto told the *Jakarta Post*, "We're also preparing snake charmers in case unexpected things happen."

High-Priced Cure

As rhinoceros horn becomes scarcer because of the dwindling number of rhinos, Chinese producers have started resorting to grinding up elaborate rhino horn carvings and antiques, some dating back to the Ming dynasty, to provide the raw ingredients for their traditional medicines. The concoctions are used to lower fevers, stop nosebleeds, and cure other minor ailments, and, contrary to popular belief, are not widely used as an aphrodisiac. Esmond Bradley Martin, a consultant with the Worldwide Fund for Nature, called the smashing of thousands of valuable works of art "a cultural tragedy akin to smashing up Renoirs to get canvas or Russian icons for matches."

Let Sleeping Dogs Lie

Amos Eugene Taylor put an electric blanket in a box on the back porch of his home in Tulsa, Oklahoma, so his dog could stay warm while it slept. During the night, a short circuit in the blanket started a fire that caused $375,000 damage.

Tough Guy

Valentin Grimaldo, of Rio Bravo, Texas, was bitten on the hand by a deadly coral snake while walking along a highway. He reacted by grabbing the snake and biting its head off, then skinning it and using the skin as a tourniquet to keep the poison from spreading.

Where's Dr. Dolittle When You Need Him?

The Agriculture Department announced that according to the Animal Welfare Act, rats, mice, and birds are not animals. As such, they are exempt from strict rules governing treatment of laboratory creatures. The Humane Society for the United States and the Animal Legal Defense Fund objected to their exclusion and sued. They won, but the department appealed. The U.S. Court of Appeals decided in favor of the Agriculture Department on a technicality: Only those directly injured by the Animal Welfare Act can sue to change it. Martin Stephens, HSUS vice president, said further appeals would be hard "unless we can teach these animals to represent themselves."

No. 1 Export

Traffic officials in Kuwait began importing wolf urine from Sweden to keep camels from colliding with cars. Sweden sprinkles the urine alongside busy mountain roads to keep elk from wandering into traffic, but Swedish researcher Rune Petterson pointed out that his field tests showed synthesized wolf urine also deters camels, which are a serious traffic hazard in parts of that Middle Eastern nation.

Rewards of Parenting without the Cost of College

• A Boston group called Helping Hands said it places baby monkeys with foster parents, who raise them for three to four years. After the monkeys become accustomed to home life and learn simple commands, they are taken from their foster homes and assigned to perform basic tasks for quadriplegics.

• In a letter urging the Utah senate to allow people to keep any pet raccoons and coyotes they have, naturalist Norinda Burbridge noted, "During the last five and one-half years, I have been attempting to teach an orphaned raccoon American sign language."

The Herd Shot round the World

Investigators for the U.S. Department of Agriculture discovered that the department was flying dairy cows around the world at taxpayers' expense. Their report to Congress on abuse, waste, and fraud in the department revealed that farmers exporting cows to take advantage of generous export subsidies flew them overseas, rather than save $18 million sending them by boat.

Tickle Me, Bossy

Researchers at the University of Maryland uncovered evidence that feeding may not be the real reason cows return to their stalls to be milked. While studying the behavior of cows being milked by robot milking machines, Mark Varner observed that the animals returned even when no food was offered. "They may just like to be milked," he said, explaining that the scientists have trouble getting the cows to leave the milker even after they've been milked.

Wretched Eggs-cess

British prosecutors described Kent toolmaker John Hemmings, 54, as a serious menace with an obsession about wild bird eggs after inspectors of the Royal Society for the Protection of Birds searched a loft in his home. They found more than 26,000 wild birds' eggs in cabinets, trays, and open drawers, as well as egg-blowing equipment. Hemmings denied taking the eggs from nests, insisting he had inherited them from a well-known collector 10 years earlier.

They Bury Horses, Don't They?

Don Blackwell arrived for work at an auto parts store in Houston and noticed two dead horses in the street, one on the median strip and the other on the shoulder. After he called the city health and solid waste departments to have the carcasses removed, a crew promptly arrived, dug a hole in the median, buried one of the horses, and left.

"Believe me, after 18 years in this business, this is one of the most bizarre things I've ever seen," said Ulysses Ford, head of the city's Solid Waste Management Department, conceding the crew did not follow standard procedure. Ford said a second crew removed the other horse from the shoulder and took it to a landfill.

Strange Reasoning

• Bradley Graff, charged with animal cruelty in Sunnyvale, California, explained that he was only trying to protect his four kittens from eye disease when he glued their eyelids closed.

• Four teenagers in Caledonia, Wisconsin, who were charged with beating a dog to death claimed they were "driven to kill something" after listening to hours of heavy-metal rock music.

Next Time, Hire a Lawyer with Lips

When David Ashley was charged with raising poultry without a permit, he appeared in court in Seneca Falls, New York, with a rooster tucked under his arm. Village Justice Gordon Tetor ordered the bird removed, but Ashley told the judge the bird was his attorney, explaining it "was the only legal counsel I could afford."

It's All Geek to Me

Boston authorities charged Joe Coleman with arson and cruelty for biting the heads off two live mice and exploding a bomb onstage. The year before, Coleman was convicted of cruelty in New York City for biting the heads off two mice.

Please Feed the Animals

Three goats and a sheep at the Southern Nevada Zoological Park in Las Vegas died of bloat because, according to zoo employees, management refused to close a profitable feed-the-animals concession on a free admission day that set an attendance record. Former keeper Jan Steele said the zoo sold 200 pounds of feed that day, four times as much as usual.

Being a Teddy Bear Is No Picnic

Australia's New South Wales state government outlawed koala-cuddling in its zoos and wildlife parks. The new rules still let people stroke and pet the marsupials, and even put their arms around one, so long as it remains on a tree branch, but they can't actually hold them. "Passing koalas around a crowd of tourists causes unacceptable stress to the animal," explained Richard Amery, the state's agriculture minister.

Australia's tourism council urged the state to reverse its decision. It explained that hugging a koala is the ultimate experience for many visitors to Australia.

Bumper Sticker Justice

The Swiss federal court ruled that drivers who brake for animals are not liable for ensuing accidents.

People Still Have to Use the Bushes

The town of Bergen-Op-Zoom in the Netherlands installed flushing sidewalk toilets for dogs.

Surprise Package

General Rudolph "Witkop" Badenhurst, head of South Africa's military intelligence during the final years of apartheid, admitted that a government-funded hit squad once planned to send a dead monkey fetus to Archbishop Desmond Tutu, but said he didn't know why.

Foxes in the Henhouse

Officials in charge of protecting China's wildlife were accused of trapping black bears and selling them to restaurants that use them either live to entertain guests or dead for bear's paw soup and other exotic dishes.

Undercover Agent

The FBI bought a horse for $5,000 to use in its investigation of race fixing at Finger Lakes Race Track in Canandaigua, New York. The horse was supposed to perform poorly to attract race fixers. Instead, Special Agent Dale Anderson said, "I can say he won at least one race and placed in about half of his races. The bureau made enough money to offset the costs of upkeep"—about $1,000 a month.

Fruits of Research

• Researchers at the University of Florida received $100,000 from the air force to fire simulated jet engines inside barns to see how the noise affects pregnant horses.

• Researchers at Louisiana State University Medical Center shot anesthetized cats in the head as part of a $2 million Defense Department study to learn how to return brain-injured soldiers to active duty.

• Australian engineers looking into the problem of birds flying into the engines of low-flying aircraft near airports decided that the best way to simulate the situation was to develop a gun that fires actual ducks into their test engines at speeds of up to 170 miles per hour. According to the trade journal *Gas Turbine News*, the engineers insisted they do not use live ducks but only ones that have first been humanely killed.

• Researchers at Harvard Medical School testing the effects of kudzu on alcohol craving chose Syrian golden hamsters for their study. Dr. Bert L. Vallee explained that this particular rodent has the unique characteristic of having a huge appetite and an alcohol consumption rate that, if scaled up to human size, would be about 40 times greater than the capacity of a typical human. After giving the hamsters alcohol-and-water cocktails to build up their tolerance, Vallee and his colleague, Wing-Ming Keung, injected some of the bingeing hamsters with compounds extracted from kudzu, a weed that is ubiquitous throughout the South. "The effect was that it reduced the alcohol intake by more than 50 percent," Vallee said, noting that the kudzu drug did not affect the hamsters' appetite for food and seemed to produce no toxicity.

• A study of ovine sexuality by University of California, Davis, graduate student Anne Perkins noted the difficulty of determining if lesbianism exists among sheep "because if you are a female sheep, what you do to solicit sex is stand still. Maybe there is a female sheep out there really wanting another female, but there's just no way for us to know it."

• In another UC study, this one at Irvine, scientists trying to determine if limbless animals use less energy than ones with legs monitored snakes slithering on treadmills wearing tiny oxygen masks.

Wild Ride

The city attorney of Carbondale, Illinois, announced he was considering filing charges against a couple who put a kitten in a bank's pneumatic deposit tube and sent it into the bank. The bank contacted police when the couple requested that the kitten, which was apparently unhurt by the first ride, be sent back to them via the tube.

Vive la Révolution!

Some 1,000 French farmers drove 300 sheep through Paris to protest lamb imports and declining prices. When police tried to control the protest, farmers began using the sheep as missiles by throwing them at the cops.

Tokens of Disaffection

• Stephanie Tubbs of Albany, New York, was charged with putting the head of a dead coyote in her ex-boyfriend's car, placing a dead squirrel on the man's doorstep, and leaving a dead cat in his hot tub.

• A woman in Jakarta, Indonesia, sought to get even with a former boyfriend by releasing six cobras into a crowded karaoke bar where the man worked.

Love Bites

Police in Moon, Pennsylvania, arrested Dennis Amber for chasing his girlfriend around her home with a 15-pound snapping turtle, trying to get the turtle to bite the woman.

Proceed to Plan B

When Pakistani stockbrokers panicked over a decline in the Karachi Stock Exchange, they sacrificed 10 black goats in an attempt to halt the drop. The goats were first paraded through the floor of the exchange and then taken outside to the parking lot to be killed. Following their deaths, the Karachi Index fell another 12.57 points.

Wonder What the Door Prize Is

A town-sponsored dance in Cabatuan, the Philippines, set the admission price at 50 rat tails. The town is at the center of the country's rice production region, and rats regularly destroy rice crops. In nearby Monpon, the city held a "Miss Rat" contest in which contestants were judged on their beauty and on the number of rats they and their sponsors had killed.

Feline-Free

Richard Evans, a member of Australia's Parliament, urged the country to adopt a policy of exterminating all cats by the year 2020. He wants a deadly virus released to kill wild cats that live in the country's outback and wants all pet cats neutered so that they will eventually die out. "I am calling for the total eradication of cats in Australia," said Evans, who blames the animals for exterminating nine native animal species in Australia.

Insects for Insects' Sake

Japanese artist Yukinori Yanagi constructed a display of sand dunes, plastic boxes, and tubes housing 5,000 ants for the Venice Biennale in 1993. The artwork was entitled *Can Art Change the World?* When animal rights activists threatened a lawsuit, Yanagi freed the ants in the gardens at the exhibition site.

Cave Canem

The Islamic fundamentalist newspaper *Jomhuri Islami* warned Tehran residents to stay away from dogs, calling them a source of psychological as well as physical illness. "The presence of dogs in the streets will leave an undesirable psychological effect on children and will cause them to be more afraid of animals," the paper declared.

Metamorphosis

A 22-year-old girl in Lahore, Pakistan, who eloped with her boyfriend, tried to stall for time by dressing a monkey in her clothes and leaving it asleep in her bed. When her parents discovered the monkey, they believed the daughter had been transformed into the animal. They tried various rituals for two days to reverse what they believed was a spell. Finally a neighbor clued them in that he had seen the girl leaving with her boyfriend.

Why Walk When You Can Drag?

• Merlin John Laing of Fairport, Iowa, was charged with animal neglect and drunk driving after police stopped him for driving with his two-year-old Pekingese dog Tippy tied to the bumper of his truck. Laing reportedly drove for two miles at speeds of up to 55 miles per hour. Tippy survived but had its side and paws rubbed raw and required surgery. Laing said that he was surprised that the dog never barked, noting, "You know how you can forget sometimes."

• Scott Theodore Eckrote of Dundalk, Maryland, was driving his car at 30 miles per hour with his Chesapeake Bay retriever Barkley running alongside, his leash hanging out a window. Neighbors called police, who went to Eckrote's home and found the dog's paw pads worn and bleeding. After Eckrote was convicted of animal cruelty, he told the court, "At the time I did it, I thought it was good. He loves to run. I thought it was healthy."

• Police in Auckland, New Zealand, were called after witnesses saw a truck dragging a cat behind it. Police found the truck parked outside a pub with the cat still attached. It had snagged its mouth on a baited fish hook hanging from the back of the truck, and the driver was totally unaware of what had happened.

Lucky Miss

When Oakland County, Michigan, prosecutor David Gorcyca charged Charles Woodworth with trying to willfully kill his dog Clementine, he explained he acted only because she was tearing up his house. His solution was to take the dog outside and shoot her in the head three times with a .32-caliber handgun. He said that he stopped because the gun "wasn't getting the job done." Clementine survived because none of the shots penetrated her skull.

Do-Gooders' Lament

After releasing 1,600 adult minks and thousands of babies from a Mount Angel, Oregon, mink farm, the Animal Liberation Front issued a statement declaring, "This action took place not as an act of 'eco-terrorism' but as an act of love." Mink industry officials responded by noting that most of the babies died from either being trampled to death, exposed to the elements, or as a result of fighting among the minks.

Just Following Directions

Park rangers at Yosemite National Park decided not to prosecute Boy Scout troop leaders who killed a bear by throwing rocks at it after an autopsy failed to prove that the rocks were the cause of death. The Scout leaders said that they "did what the brochure told us" in throwing rocks at the bear to scare it away from food at their campsite. Rangers said that the brochure would be rewritten to specify that only small stones the size of golf balls or smaller should be used. The rocks used by the Scout leaders were as big as softballs.

Passing the Time

British Royal Air Force pilots stationed in the Falkland Islands developed a game they play with the local penguin population, according to a Mexican news report. After noticing that the birds seem entranced by the jets flying overhead, the pilots began looking for beaches loaded with penguins and flew slowly past along the coast. Thousands of penguins appear to turn their heads in unison as the jets pass overhead.

The pilots then turn around and fly back in the opposite direction and watch as the heads turn that way. Next the pilots fly out over the ocean and return directly toward the penguins, which forces them to look up and, continuing to keep pace with the planes overhead, look farther back until they fall over. The RAF denied the report.

Special Section: If I Could Be Like the Animals

Embraceable Ewe

Economist Brian Easton suggested at a conference on child rearing in Dunedin, New Zealand, that one way New Zealand families might be able to afford to raise children is to register them as sheep. That way, he said, the children's food, accommodation, and other expenses would be tax deductible.

Justice Served

After years of complaining about their neighbors' constantly barking dogs, the Hills family in Kittery, Maine, finally convinced the authorities to take action. But police issued the first summons to the Hillses' son, Henry Paradis, for creating a nuisance by barking back at the dogs.

Dutch Treat

Art & Antiques magazine noted that at the opening of Amsterdam's Katten Kabinet, the only museum devoted to cats, human guests "munched dainty slices of toast spread with cucumbers, tomatoes and a pâté, later said to actually have been cat food."

Don't Know Why the Caged Bird Sings

Four men who accepted a $15,000 challenge from British animal rights activist Rebecca Hall to live like hens in a cold, cramped cage for a week lasted just 18 hours. The cage, which had no sanitation facilities, measured three feet square and just over six feet high, duplicating what Hall called "animal concentration camps" used to produce cheap chickens. Richard Brett, one of the four men who failed the challenge, said, "I feel stiff, sore, and knackered [worn out], and was not enormously disappointed when they unlocked the door."

Great Pretender

Impersonating an animal worked for Darrell Stair, a police officer in Kelso, Washington. When his partner, Officer Ernie Moore, told a 42-year-old assault suspect holed up in his attic to come down or a dog would be sent up, Stair barked and growled like a dog. The suspect immediately surrendered.

Carbon Copy

Ruth Durbin spied a parakeet in a tree in Nailsea, England, who announced, "I'm Pippy. I live at number seven Strawberry Close, Nailsea—got that?" Durbin went to the address about half a mile away and left a note for the owner, Arthur Bendon. "Later, I got a phone call from Mr. Bendon, which stopped me in my tracks," Durbin explained. "His voice was exactly the same as the bird's."

FUR FIGHTS BACK

Animals Looking
for Revenge

Labor Dispute

A monkey in Kota Bahru, Malaysia, that had been trained to climb palm trees, pick coconuts, and drop them to his owner below, instead threw a coconut at the owner, Mat Hussin Sulaiman, hitting him in the neck and killing him.

Snap-Happy

Police officers, firefighters, and animal control officers were needed to rescue a woman trapped in her Savannah, Georgia, home by a 12-inch snapping turtle. According to police, each time the woman tried to leave her house, the turtle snapped at her.

Saboteurs

• An express train in Morocco was halted near Meknes, 87 miles north of the capital of Rabat, when snails swarmed onto the rails and their slime caused the train's wheels to lose their grip. The newspaper *Opinion* reported that the snails had appeared in great numbers because of heavy rain and that for some unknown reason they often congregate at that spot on the Casablanca-Fez line.

• Japanese police investigating a series of train mishaps

identified the culprits as crows. A surveillance camera caught one bird placing an egg-size rock on the tracks. Authorities said crows are responsible for three cases of stones being placed on tracks. "I cannot tell if the crow was expecting to cause this chaos," bird expert Koichi Karasawa, the author of a book called *Why the Crow Is So Smart*, said after viewing the police video, explaining, "It looked as if the crow was just playing, enjoying trying to put the stones on the rail."

Cyberworm

Susie Garner, 31, a public relations assistant at Keefe University in Newcastle-under-Lyme, England, finally discovered what made her computer crash: an earthworm in the hard drive. "Every time the worm wriggled," she explained, "the computer shut itself down again."

Water Hazards

• Charles Calhoun II was riding a Jet Ski in the ocean off North Carolina when a Spanish mackerel jumped out of the water, over the handlebars, and bit him on the neck.

• Fiji fisherman Kinijioji Vindovi, 69, was asleep in his fishing boat with four other fishermen when a shark leapt into the boat and attacked and killed him.

• Chris Browne, a New Zealand skin diver, speared a 295-pound striped marlin in a fishing contest and was towed for three miles out to sea by the wounded fish before it eventually tired.

• Bobby Martin, 47, was watching friends fish from a charter boat in the Gulf of Mexico near Bradenton, Florida, when a 40-pound barracuda leaped out of the water, sailed over the captain's head, landed on Martin mouth first, knocking the strapping construction supervisor off a bench and tearing open his left arm, requiring 24 stitches.

The next day, Nadine Cloer was fishing with her family off the Florida Keys when her brother-in-law hooked a five-foot barracuda. As she moved closer with a video camera, an eight-foot barracuda shot over the boat railing and locked onto her arm with its razor-sharp teeth. "It was like a torpedo," said Cloer after receiving nearly 200 stitches. "It looked like it was diving straight for me."

• When Mitsuya Nakajima, 41, was found dead off the coast of Japan's Oshima Island with a stab wound to the neck, authorities found a light used underwater for night fishing and concluded that Nakajima was killed by a needlefish. The species features a very sharp beak that can grow to more than 10 centimeters—about the depth of the victim's stab wound—and, like many fish, is attracted to lights at night.

• While ice fishing on a reservoir 60 miles northwest of Moscow, a man who caught a 28-inch pike showed it to his fellow fishermen by raising it to his mouth and kissing it. The fish, known for its many teeth, clamped down on the man's nose. Its jaws stayed locked even after the angler's friends beheaded it, requiring them to take him to a hospital, where doctors finally removed the fish's head.

• Nathon do Nascimento was fishing in a Brazilian river near the remote Amazon city of Belem when a six-inch-long fish suddenly leapt out of the river and into his mouth, lodging in his throat. Two other fishermen tried to help him, but by the time they got him to a local hospital, he was dead.

Misguided Missiles

• A flock of Canada geese struck a U.S. Air Force AWACS radar plane at Elmendorf Air Force Base near Anchorage, Alaska, jamming two of the plane's four engines and sending it crashing to the ground, killing all 24 aboard.

• A flock of birds collided with a national guard reconnaissance fighter jet over Idaho, blasting a hole in the plane's canopy and hitting the pilot in the shoulder. The weapons officer managed to land the plane safely.

Picture This

Michio Hoshino, a wildlife photographer known for his photos of bears, was mauled to death by a brown bear while filming a documentary on Russia's Kamchatka Peninsula. Hoshino was asleep in his tent when the bear attacked and dragged his body into the forest.

Tracks of Her Tears

A mother grizzly bear stopped train traffic across northern Montana after two of her cubs were struck and killed by a freight train in the early morning hours. The mother proceeded to charge all other trains in the dark until service was halted.

Never Forget

A mother elephant, enraged that a villager in West Bengal, India, had beaten one of its babies to death for rampaging through his house, returned and trampled the man to death.

It's All Happening at the Zoo

• Carlos Alberto Oliveira Fontes, 47, entered the zoo in Salvador, Brazil, and deliberately stuck his arm into the lion cage to "test the power of God," according to police and his mother. The lion ripped off his arm, and Fontes was taken to a hospital. His mother told police that he earlier said, "If God is so powerful, he will not allow the lion to hurt me."

• Prakesh Tiwari was killed and Suresh Rai injured at the Calcutta zoo on New Year's Day after they decided to put a marigold garland around the neck of a 13-year-old male Royal Bengal tiger in celebration of the holiday. The two men, who authorities said had been drinking, entered the tiger's enclosure by crossing a moat.

• Two Manchurian brown bears mauled Matthew Settles, 28, after he jumped into their enclosure at the San Diego Zoo.

Zoo workers had to use high-pressure hoses to scare away the bears, but not before they slashed Settles in the groin. At the hospital afterward, he told police that he was sure the bears had "motioned for him to join them."

• Fumanekile Ngqase, 27, climbed into the tiger cage at the Queen's Park Zoo in East London, South Africa, pulled a knife, and tried to provoke the tigers into attacking. He suffered only a few scratches before zookeepers arrived to rescue him. According to zoo officials, Ngqase said that he "wanted to die in style by fighting tigers."

• The orangutans at the San Diego Zoo caused $57,000 in damage by using rocks to shatter seven windows separating them from zoo visitors. The six-by-seven-foot windows are three layered and one and a half inches thick, weigh more than 900 pounds, and require eight men to lift them. Zoo workers had previously worked out a system in which they took rocks from the animals by offering them bananas instead. However, zoo officials noted that the animals got wise to the situation and began to hoard rocks to use to trade for the fruit. The zoo's spokeswoman noted that the zoo has tried to conduct the trades more often and said that the orangutans like to throw things and regularly dig holes looking for rocks.

Flipped Its Lid

Becky Kelly found a monkey in a friend's backyard in Hollidaysburg, Pennsylvania, took it home, and put it in a cage. The monkey was apparently calm until the next day when, let out to play, it looked through a window and saw two men approach the house. "It went nuts," said another woman who lived in the house. The monkey grabbed a paring knife from the kitchen and a cigarette lighter and went on a rampage through the home for two hours, running and screaming and trying to flick the lighter on. It bit two women and used the knife to slice open bags of food in the kitchen cupboards, stopping to eat marshmallows, sugar, and bread. Police were unable to subdue it, and animal control officers had to be called in to snare the animal.

Political Commentary

Elections for Nigeria's national assembly in Lagos had to be canceled after a dozen chimpanzees attacked the presiding electoral officer as he was walking to the polling station.

Worse Than Teenagers

Japanese authorities reported that more than 350 wild chickens living in the park in front of the city hall in Hiratsuka regularly attack passers-by, pecking at their legs and attacking children. Butchers declined to take them, and the local public health department refused to round them up and remove them.

Determined Aggression

• A stray cat attacked Bonni Matheson outside her home in Davenport, Washington. After scratching and biting her hands, it ran up a tree. Later it attacked her two teenage sons. Finally police arrived and used a skunk trap to capture the cat. Police took it to a veterinary office for a 10-day-long rabies observation process, but the cat escaped after only two days and immediately returned to the Matheson house. "It went right after us," said Bonni Matheson, who had just returned from the hospital. It then ran inside the house, tore wallpaper in the kitchen, and attacked the three family dogs in the living room. Eventually the cat was caged and later destroyed.

• Two huge rottweiler dogs entered the Greenmart Live Poultry store in Flushing, New York, herded the employees into a backroom, then proceeded to feast on the live chickens, spending more than an hour chasing and eating a couple dozen birds. The carnage stopped when a SWAT team showed up with dart guns to subdue the dogs.

• Troops of rampaging baboons began regularly throwing rocks at cars along South Africa's busy N1 highway. According to news reports, police engaged the baboons in "running battles" in an attempt to get them to leave.

Monkey Business

• Gangs of wild monkeys began raiding the apple orchards in the western suburbs of Tokyo, picking and eating apples and even taking some with them. Reports said, "Some monkeys were seen carrying apples away in plastic shopping bags."

• Japanese macaque monkeys have become so numerous that they now invade cities to ransack homes and stores for food. During the 1970s the government, in an attempt to draw tourists to the countryside, built havens for the wild monkeys. Now they are blamed for destroying 150,000 acres of crops per year and for numerous incidents in which they have entered stores and taken candy bars, fruit, and vegetables right off the shelves. The cities of Hakone and Odawara built a $2 million preserve for the monkeys outside of the two cities to deter the urban attacks, but the monkeys shunned it.

• A 66-year-old woman in Suffolk County, New York, was waiting for a ride to church one Sunday morning when her doorbell rang. She looked out the window to see two rhesus monkeys standing on the porch, ringing her doorbell, knocking on the door, and trying to turn the doorknob. The woman called the police, who said the pair had escaped from their cages in their owner's house and gotten out of the house.

• Edna Bradley, 78, of Inman, South Carolina, was hanging sheets on a clothesline when a chimpanzee that escaped from the Hollywild Animal Park knocked her down and proceeded to roll her around like a ball. According to Bradley, after several minutes she was able to get free, but the chimp "grabbed me up again and rolled me over and over. I was just being rolled and tumbled every which way." She finally got inside her house and called 911 while the chimp stood at her porch door. The animal, one of three escaped chimps, was later captured. The owner of the animal park explained that when Mrs. Bradley was standing hanging clothes, the position of her hands over her head was seen as an aggressive stance from the chimp's point of view. "He likes women," the owner insisted. "He wasn't trying to hurt her. He thought it was funny, rolling this lady around on the ground."

• Five years after a south Texas primate shelter imported 150 free-breeding Japanese snow monkeys, 600 of them escaped because the facility couldn't come up with $105,000 to fix the electric fence around its 58 acres. The primates continued breeding and began running wild around Dilley, Texas, stealing groceries, destroying crops, and damaging homes and cars (including taking radio antennas from trucks). In one case the entire group of monkeys descended onto the roof of a single ranch house, where they stayed for a year despite efforts to move them along. "There was poo-poo everywhere," one family member said. "You can just imagine what it is like to have 600 monkeys running around on your roof." Another rancher tried to keep the monkeys away from her home by placing rubber snakes around the house, but the monkeys used them as jump ropes.

• Officials in India preparing for parliamentary elections had to hire a private security firm to protect election offices from further attacks by hordes of roving monkeys that ripped the curtains off voting booths and intimidated workers. Fearing they might cause further damage, Delhi's Chief Electoral Officer T. T. Joseph said the security agency was considering using sprays to immobilize the monkeys and air guns to scare them away.

• Armed vigilantes outside Dhaka, Bangladesh, launched a search for a monkey that slapped, bit, and scratched scores of people, sending 13 of them to the hospital. One group showed support for the monkey, organizing a street demonstration. Members of Youths for Animals carried signs reading WE ARE READY TO DIE FOR THE FREEDOM OF THE MONKEY.

• Monkeys began terrorizing residents of a remote Philippine island, raiding their village for food, then fleeing to nearby caves with their spoils. Governor Romero Salalima of Albay said people on Bataan Island complained that the monkeys also have raided crops and fish harvests, consuming "practically everything in sight." Witnesses reported that the raiders are an endangered species that normally grows no taller than two feet, but they are led by a monkey "the size of a first grader."

• When a noisy construction crew woke up chimpanzees at a wild animal park in southern France, eight of the chimps attacked the workers, mauling one of the men so badly that he needed 30 stitches in his face and neck. Another worker escaped by jumping into a pond, and five other park employees hid in a walk-in freezer until the animals were subdued.

Dizzy with Dismay

A rabid skunk chased Carmen LaBrecque around the outside of her house in Salem, Massachusetts, for 15 minutes. Since the skunk was always just a few steps behind, the woman was unable to stop to open the door. During one pass, her mother handed her a cell phone. She dialed 911, and an animal control officer responded by shooting the skunk. LaBrecque and the skunk had circled the house 12 times.

Hide Your Woolens

A swarm of moths swarmed over a bridge in northern Japan, creating a half-inch-deep mass that caused 19 cars to skid out of control.

Revenge of Caddyshack

• Three janitors at an elementary school in Ceres, California, tried to freeze a gopher to death by spraying it with a solvent that freezes gum and wax so it can be peeled or chipped away. Jeff Davis, 35, said he and his colleagues had sprayed several cans of the gum remover on the gopher inside a small, poorly ventilated utility room with the doors closed when one of them tried to light a cigarette. Sparks from the lighter ignited the solvent, causing an explosion that blew the janitors out of the utility room, sending them and 16 pupils to the hospital. The gopher survived and was later released in a field. Ceres Unified School District Superintendent Bruce Newlin commented that the men "used extraordinarily poor judgment."

• A gopher chewing through a fiber-optic cable disabled long-distance telephone service for 6,800 U.S. West customers in New Mexico. Among the other casualties were 911 service and control tower communications at two airports.

Playing with Fire

Matthew Gould awoke to find his home in Kelso, Washington, on fire. He called firefighters who extinguished the fire and discovered that it had been caused by Gould's five-month-old dog chewing on a box of matches. "We've been talking about getting rid of her for a while now," Gould said, "and this kind of put it over the top."

Behind You!

Kyle Thompson, a Seffner, Florida, teenager, accused his cat of shooting him in the back. He explained that he was cleaning a closet and placed his .22-caliber rifle on his bed. He said there was a round in the chamber and that the cat must have jumped on the rifle or walked over it, causing it to fire.

Hugs and Hisses

• Mary Anne Carter awoke one morning at her San Diego home to find the family pet, a nine-foot-long Burmese python, wrapping itself around her stomach and biting her buttocks. Carter was eight months pregnant at the time. Her husband, Brad, tried to free her from the snake's grip with a small knife, but the snake ensnared him, too. A neighbor arrived with a crowbar, and both men tried to get the snake's mouth off Mary Anne's buttocks, but to no avail. Finally paramedics arrived and sawed the snake's head off. "It was more like a puppy dog than a snake," Brad said afterward. "It would follow you around the house. For some reason, it woke up and felt it needed to attack." He added that his wife had never wanted a snake in the house and let him have one only after he begged her for years.

• A 12-foot-long python in Anaheim, California, attacked its owner, a 10-year-old boy, biting his hand and wrapping its body twice around the boy's arm. The boy's brother tried in vain to make the snake let go by stabbing it with a steak knife. Paramedics arrived and used a large knife to cut the snake's head off.

• Timothy Sickles, 28, of Clifton, New Jersey, lifted the top of his pet python's tank to give it water when the snake leapt at him, bit his face, and wrapped itself around his neck, still biting his face. Timothy's sister heard his screams and first tried cutting the snake off with a knife. When she realized it wasn't sharp enough she grabbed a butcher knife and hacked through the python's neck. While its body slithered away, the head remained clamped on her brother's head. Once they pried it off and threw it down, the snake's jaws continued to bite.

• Grant Williams, 19, of New York City died when his 13-foot-long, 44-pound pet Burmese python crushed his neck. According to his neighbors, Williams often walked around the neighborhood with the python wrapped around his neck.

The snake was fed a live chicken or rabbit every few weeks, and police found a live chicken loose in Williams's apartment. "The snake was trained," Williams's brother said. "We trusted that snake. I never thought it would hurt any of us."

Spoilsports

Two hours before the start of an Easter-egg hunt in Juneau, Alaska, organizers went out in a field to hide more than 1,000 hard-boiled eggs and some plastic ones containing candy. When the children arrived and began registering for the hunt, dozens of crows and ravens descended on the field and began stealing the real eggs and opening the plastic ones to get at the candy.

Out of This World

The launch of the space shuttle *Discovery* was delayed five days in 1995 after NASA found that two woodpeckers had made 135 holes in the insulating foam of the fuel tank. Technicians had to remove the spacecraft from its launching pad to repair the damage. When the countdown finally began, ground controllers played Woody Woodpecker's signature laugh for the astronauts.

Is That a Live Animal on Your Lap, Or . . . ?

Health officials in Toronto stopped the movie and evacuated a downtown theater just after a raccoon looking for food bit a man eating popcorn.

Ear Raid

An invasion of miller moths caused a rash of injuries in Boulder County, Colorado, mostly broken fingers and injured shoulders caused by people swatting the harmless but annoying pests. In a more serious incident, a miller moth landed on a 46-year-old man's head and crawled into his ear. The man couldn't get the moth out and was forced to call for help. An ambulance company spokesperson said that when rescuers arrived the man was trying to suck the moth out with "a vacuum attached to his ear."

The Pause That Refreshes

Korean cab driver Choe Pyong Gil, 43, stopped at one of Seoul's dog-meat restaurants for a meal. When he opened the door to what he thought was a toilet, the special of the day, still alive, bit Choe's leg.

Whoopee!

Police in Westerville, Ohio, formed special patrols to search for a squirrel that appears friendly but attacks adults and chases children. An official said that at least eight victims told him the squirrel approaches, then "just zooms up your leg like it was a tree."

Let It Be

Police in Santa Rosa, California, reported that Gary Bowers had been bothered by woodpeckers and tried using a pellet gun to drive them away. Unsuccessful, he bought a shotgun. The first time he went to use it, he slipped on his front porch on the way to his targets, and the gun fired, killing him.

Rocky Raccoons

A colony of raccoons, brought to Germany from North America 60 years ago, escaped from the Wolfshagen Fur Farm when it was bombed by the Allies in 1945. With no natural enemies, the raccoon population has increased to more than 100,000, raising fears among residents, especially farmers, who complained that the animals raid henhouses and gnaw through electricity cables.

Pushy Americans

Louisiana crawfish, imported by Spain in the 1960s to appeal to the national palate, today are devouring the country's rice fields. The regional government of Catalonia declared the mudbugs a plague and instructed the agriculture department to use all means to destroy them. Farmers tried gassing them, with no luck, then began using pesticides to eradicate the crawfish, which are twice the size of the native species, more resistant to pollution, and according to biologist Raul Escosa, "have a high reproductive level" and no predators. "I don't know exactly where Louisiana is," said rice farmer Juan Tiron, "but I wish the people there would come and take them back."

Another Nail in Its Coffin

The National Cancer Institute complained that the northern spotted owl is preventing it from obtaining 720,000 pounds of tree bark needed to produce 55 pounds of a compound being tested against cancer. The drug, Taxol, has shown promise against ovarian cancer, which claims 12,000 victims a year, and is being tested against breast, lung, and colon cancers. The institute said the only tree that produces the right bark is the Pacific yew, but harvesting that much bark would mean going into forests set aside as sanctuaries for the owl, a threatened species whose survival in turn threatens the Pacific Northwest's timber industry.

Sneak Attack

Charlie Jackson Coleman, 61, was walking alongside a rural road outside Caldwell, Texas, when a 160-pound deer with eight-point antlers attacked, gored, and fatally trampled him. The buck was still standing over Coleman's body hours later when deputies arrived and shot it after it attacked them. An autopsy found more than 100 hoof and puncture wounds on Coleman's back, stomach, and face.

Cat Food

A reclusive man who loved cats was eaten by his 15 pets after he died, leaving them without food, according to police in Leiden, Netherlands, who were alerted by neighbors who hadn't seen the 69-year-old man for two weeks. Police spokesperson Robert Blom said officers found the remains of Frans Heemskerk "almost totally eaten up" by his cats.

Another Argument for Vegetarianism

A cow that escaped from a slaughterhouse in Jundiai, Brazil, injured four people while running through the streets before crashing through a hospital fence. Police had to fire six shots to kill it, but their bullets also wounded two hospital workers.

Hide the Highway

• Pest control experts in California, Louisiana, Florida, Tennessee, and Hawaii reported sighting the Formosan termite, a ferociously aggressive species that has been known to eat not just wood but also asphalt, concrete, and metal. According to Vernard Lewis, an entomologist at the University of California at Berkeley, the bugs, which originated in China, tend to nest in huge colonies that can number in the tens of millions.

• Microscopic animals are stripping the asphalt off highways, according to Mississippi State University biology professor Lewis Brown, who warned, "We've shown in our lab experiments that the microbes strip the asphalt right off the rocks in the asphalt mix."

A Decade with Taste

Termites have eaten through half of the government buildings in Jakarta, according to M. Pasaribu, who oversees government construction and maintenance in Indonesia, where

200 different types of termites eat not just wood but also concrete, brick, metal plates, and plastic pipes. Pasaribu told the *Jakarta Post* that the termites seemed especially fond of structures built in the 1970s.

Run Away! Run Away!

• Giant mutant rats invaded a suburb of Santiago, Chile, alarming farmers and attacking chickens and small goats, according to the independent news agency Orbe. Environmentalist Maurico Barraza, president of the Ecological Council of Maipu, said the two-foot-long rodents grew that large by eating the droppings of hormone-fattened poultry.

• Officials in the northeastern Chinese city of Benxi reported a column of migrating toads more than 1,000 miles long winding through Liaoning province. The government news agency Xinhua said most of the toads were newly born and no longer than a fingernail, but larger ones spaced out every 30 feet appeared to be leading the others.

• Blind kangaroos are stumbling around southeastern Australia. Unable to explain the cause, officials said that since ranchers and farmers around the remote New South Wales mining town of Broken Hill first reported kangaroos behaving oddly, the affliction spread rapidly, blinding at least a tenth of the 500,000 western gray kangaroos in southeastern Australia and 2.8 million in New South Wales.

Paper Chase

Monkeys attacked a government office in Tezpur, India, drove officials away, and spent 25 minutes destroying documents.

Crazy Rodents

• After a squirrel attacked a woman at a real estate office in Kirkland, Washington, police caught it and put it in a plastic cage while a veterinarian checked it for rabies. The squirrel gnawed through the cage, then held more than 50 workers in the office at bay before escaping.

• Authorities at California's Concord Naval Weapons Station warned that an army of squirrels was threatening the base's safety by digging tunnels that weaken safety structures designed to withstand accidental explosions, creating a potential hazard. Spokesperson Dan Tikalsky added that the squirrels also burrowed beneath roads in a 5,000-acre part of the facility.

For the Birds

• A woman in Thrissur, India, accused her neighbor of stealing her pet parrot. The neighbor also claimed to own the bird. The judge ruled for the plaintiff when the bird squawked the names of its owner's children.

• After more than 20,000 rooks besieged the Dutch village of Witharen, citizens complained that the constant noise and droppings were making their lives stressful. "Our cars, bicycles, and washing are always covered in bird droppings," one villager lamented. "It looks as if snow has just fallen." Because rooks are a protected species in the Netherlands and may not be shot, teams of firefighters hosed away the nests with water cannons. Within a couple of days, the rooks returned. Controlled explosions proved no more effective; the rooks became used to the booms and simply ignored them. Hans Peeters, spokesperson for the Dutch Bird Protection Society, advised Witharen residents "to try to live in harmony with their rook neighbors and get to know their fascinating ways."

• Hundreds of birds flew down a chimney and into the living room of a house in Port Angeles, Washington, leaving a mess of soot and feathers covered with bird droppings. "It was exactly like [Alfred Hitchcock's movie] *The Birds*, except they didn't attack people," said Chris Thomas, who was at home with her husband and their son. A fire rescue team arrived and collected the birds, then released them outside, but the birds circled the house and flew back down the chimney. Finally, they placed a board over the chimney to keep the birds from returning.

What's Up Down Under

• In Australia, a kookaburra whose nesting tree was cut down for a building extension repeatedly dive-bombed Hastings District Hospital. The bird smashed three windows and damaged a laser photocopier.

• Also in Australia, grasshoppers forced Elton John to flee a Melbourne concert stage in 1993. The invading insects landed in the British singer's hair, clothes, and mouth, and crawled over backup singers and musical instruments. Concert publicist Patti Mostyn said she was surprised the singer lasted almost two hours before walking off the stage, which had become so slick with crushed, oozing insects that "backing singers started to slip."

Yikes!

A 70-year-old woman was killed when she was attacked by at least four alligators at a lake in the Wildwood, Florida, retirement community where she lived. Bill Farmer, a Sumter County sheriff's deputy, said the dismembered body of Grace Eberhart was found after neighbors reported alligators "playing with what appeared to be a human body." Farmer said authorities did not rule out suicide, explaining that Eberhart was killed by a bite to the head, but there were no drag marks on the bank of the lake and no bite marks on her feet or lower legs. "She would have had to have been prone," Farmer said, "or up to her neck in the water for them to grab her head and neck."

Turnabout Is Fair Play

Constable Laurie McNeal sent a police dog into a house in Timaru, New Zealand, to disarm a man carrying a gun. When the dog gripped the man's arm, the man bit off part of the dog's ear. McNeal said the dog responded by letting go of the arm and biting the man's testicles, ending his resistance.

Fallout

Melany Paula Campos, 60, who shared a home in Los Angeles with her sister and some 40 dogs, was found dead beneath four large bags of dog food. Scott Carrier of the coroner's office said the heavy bags apparently smothered Campos.

Manly Man

After Wayne Roth of Pittston, Pennsylvania, was bitten by a cobra belonging to his friend, Roger Croteau, he refused to go to the hospital, telling Croteau, "I'm a man, I can handle it." Instead, Roth went to a bar, where he had a few drinks and boasted to other patrons about the incident. He died a few hours later.

How Do You Break a Bleeding Heart?

Seven years after world opinion forced a halt to Canada's annual clubbing of baby harp seals in 1983, the seal population had rebounded to an estimated 4 million. Fishermen in Newfoundland and Nova Scotia complained the seals were overrunning their fishing grounds, eating valuable and increasingly scarce fish, and damaging nets and aquaculture projects. The fishermen proposed that the government let them cull the gray and harp seal herds and subsidize the hunt, since prices for pelts had fallen from $21 to about $5. They also volunteered to feed the remaining seals contraceptives.

Bee In

In Brazil, an estimated 50,000 "killer bees" swarmed into a Rio de Janeiro subway station, attacking passengers on platforms and in trains. Police said the attack, which killed one person and injured 100 others, occurred when a watchman at a nearby construction site started up a tractor near the bees' hive, apparently making enough noise to irritate them.

Playing Possum

After John K. Riley Sr., 38, of Long Bottom, Ohio, ran over a deer, he got out to inspect the damage to his car. Riley told the Meigs County Sheriff's Department that the deer, which had been lying with its back to him but apparently wasn't killed, then got up, butted him into a nearby creek, and left the scene.

Where's Our Share of the Royalties?

The author of *All Creatures Great and Small* and other tales of a British country veterinarian was hospitalized in Yorkshire, England, after being attacked by a flock of sheep. James Herriot, whose real name is Alf Wight, 77, was trying to stop the sheep from grazing on his lawn when they butted and trampled him, breaking his leg.

Lights Out

Polar bears on Alaska's Barter Island keep bashing landing lights on a runway until they go out. Naturalists who have investigated the behavior cannot explain it.

Where's the Pied Piper When You Need Him?

• Norwegian authorities had to gas more than 1,000 rats that took over the house of an Oslo couple who had been breeding them to sell to a pet shop. The shop went bankrupt, police officer Klaus Henning Os explained, but the couple decided to keep a few unsold rats, including a pregnant female, who subsequently escaped her cage. Soon the house was filled with rats roaming freely, gnawing the furniture and forcing the couple to move out. "The man has personal problems and lost control," Os said. "Instead of seeking help, he started feeding the rats."

• The rat problem in Bangladesh got even worse after the government began holding twice-yearly rat-killing campaigns and awarding prizes, such as color televisions, to whoever collects the most rat tails. Prize-minded contestants poured on their fields and food storage units powerful pesticides that scarcely affect the rat population but that destroy snakes, owls, and other predators of rats.

• When landlord Per Hatlen went to the house he had rented to a 44-year-old man and his wife in Vestby, Norway, he found the couple had gone, but they left behind more than 1,000 rats. The renter, who was reported to be in hiding, told police he liked rats and wanted to breed them for pet stores, but the situation just got out of control.

• Traffic in the Greek capital of Athens was snarled by mice and rats gnawing through traffic light cables. City officials added that the traffic jams were compounded by maintenance workers, who knocked out many of the signal lights with high-pressure water hoses they were using to wash off accumulated pigeon droppings.

• Honduras launched a campaign to eliminate rats from hospitals after 13 patients died in Tegucigalpa when rats chewing on electrical wires caused a short circuit in the intensive care unit of the Mario Catarino Rivasto hospital. The short circuit stopped respirators and other life-maintaining equipment.

• The Ernesto Cortissoz airport in Barranquilla, Colombia, shut down for nearly an hour after a rat caused a short circuit by urinating on a high-power cable, knocking out communications between the control tower and incoming aircraft.

• Christina and Cliff Fields had to call police after their 300 pet rats took over their condo in San Carlos, California. The rodents, some a foot long, ate through the Sheetrock, started nesting in the walls, and got into the cabinets. Christina Fields explained that she and Cliff started with three rats, but one of them turned out to be pregnant. After that, she said, things just got out of hand.

• In Lanesboro, Minnesota, Lyle Harlos, 37, tried to kill a rat living in his garage by gassing it with carbon monoxide from his car exhaust. According to Olmsted County Coroner Paul Belau, fumes seeped into the house from the attached garage and killed Harlos.

• Terri Fulton filed a $250,000 suit against a Holiday Inn near Dayton, Ohio. She said while spending the night there she noticed "another creature in bed with her" that turned out to be a big rat "eating my buttock."

• Ray Santos, a candidate for state representative in Maranhao, Brazil, was campaigning on television when a rat bit him. He grabbed the rat by the tail and held it up to the camera, announcing, "Starting now, we begin our campaign against rats." Santos, who later received eight antirabies injections, vowed that once elected he would distribute rat traps to everyone in the state.

• After moving into a new office in Santa Rosa, California, architect Betty Crawford said she went into the rest room, and an eight-inch rat jumped out of the toilet and onto her lap. "I just yelled and jumped up," Crawford said. "I began to chase him, and he jumped on me three or four times as I tried to shoo him out the door." City utilities director Miles Ferris said there are about a dozen reports a year of rats in people's yards, sewer lines, and toilets.

• Prime Minister Phan Van Khai ordered restaurants in Vietnam to stop serving cat meat after a wave of catnapping reduced the domestic cat population, which then accelerated crop damage caused by the country's rapidly growing rat population. In addition, the Agriculture Ministry encouraged people to switch from eating cats and snakes to eating rats instead.

This Cheshire Cat Isn't Smiling

Police in Cheshire, Connecticut, had to use pepper spray to subdue a cat who attacked a woman in a wheelchair at her home. Helena Roach, 46, explained she suffered bites and cuts on her legs when she accidentally ran over the cat's tail with her wheelchair.

Just Deserts

A man walked into a Houston pet store and tried to sell owner Shawn Cochran two rattlesnakes. When Cochran explained that city law banned the store from selling poisonous reptiles, the man grabbed seven pythons, ran to his pickup truck, and sped off. Cochran gave chase and collided with the thief, who was bitten by one of the rattlesnakes when his truck rolled over.

Don't Have a Cow

• Timotea Soriano, 82, was playing cards with three friends at her home in Viver, Spain, when a bull crashed through her front door, gored her, and hurled her against the wall, injuring her fatally. Authorities explained that the bull had escaped from a temporary bullring set up in the village square as part of Viver's annual festival.

• Two bulls escaped from a pasture in Houston and were wandering around on a road when a car hit them. Both bulls were severely injured. One collapsed in a ditch, but the second charged police officers, who fired more than 40 shots, hitting it at least two dozen times and emptying their service revolvers without stopping it. Finally a sheriff's deputy arrived with a rifle, taking three shots to fell the bull.

• John Hine, 55, was crossing a field near Tetsworth, England, when a herd of dairy cows attacked him, breaking his leg and badly bruising his chest.

Thanks for Nothing

A Latin American beetle that turned up in relief food sent to Africa to fight starvation immediately threatened to devastate food supplies in 10 nations. The greater grain borer, or scania beetle, not only destroys most stored produce, but it even eats wooden utensils and storage sheds.

Don't Fence Us In

Residents of Mada Island, a mile off Kenya in the Indian Ocean, reported that elephants from the mainland swam across the channel, then uprooted coconut palms, mango orchards, and other crops on the island. Authorities tried to calm the farmers by explaining that the island has been on the elephants' regular migration route for centuries.

Sweet Revenge

Students at the University of Alaska harassed a moose and her calf by throwing snowballs, yelling, whistling, and shouting at them for hours as they roamed the Anchorage campus. The agitated animals were outside the gym when Myong Chin Ra, 71, arrived to use the sauna. Witnesses said Ra tried to sneak by, but the moose charged. Ra ran but slipped, and the moose stomped him to death.

One Hung Low

Singapore's former discus and shot put champion Fok Keng Choy was sitting on his toilet, according to Malaysia's *New Straits Times*, when a python bit his testicles.

There's Gratitude for You

British animal rights activist Vicki Moore, 39, was hospitalized in serious condition after being gored nine times during a bull-running festival in Coria, Spain. A half-ton bull attacked her while she was filming a documentary about how the bulls are mistreated.

Elephant Burial Grounds

Angry elephants trampled a Namibian youth to death in South Africa and buried him in the sand, leaving only a shoe to mark where he died. Police Inspector Werner Gevers said the body "was found some distance away, buried under sand that had been stamped down. A branch was found on top of the spot."

Chow Time

An elephant at Hrodno zoo in western Belarus attacked and killed a 42-year-old keeper because he was angry that she was an hour late bringing his lunch.

Revenge of Moby Dick

After the Norwegian whaling boat *Boga* harpooned a minke whale off Norway's northern coast, the whale rammed the vessel, toppling its mast and tossing two crew members into the icy water. The Oslo newspaper *Verdens Gang* reported the crew members were rescued and the whale escaped.

Meals on the Run

Lions in South Africa's Kruger National Park began attacking and eating illegal immigrants crossing the nearby border from Mozambique, according to park rangers, who told local newspapers that the lions have discovered that people taste good and make easy prey.

The Ghost of Mr. Chicken

Kay Martin, a New Zealand secretary, was cooking dinner while she and a friend talked, when they heard a chicken squawking as if in distress. They looked outside but saw nothing. Then Martin realized the sound was coming from her own oven, where she was roasting a stuffed chicken. She removed the bird, which ceased squawking, and cut off its neck. After noticing its vocal cords were intact, Martin reckoned that steam from the stuffing was coming up the neck and causing the sound. "It was as if it was shrieking at me from its grave," she told the Auckland *Sunday Star*. "It was so bizarre I just froze."

Hair Triggers

After a dog tied to a post began barking late at night in Yekaterinburg, Russia, neighbors complained to police. According to the daily paper *Izvestia*, three officers who responded decided to shoot the dog. They fired nine times, missing the dog but hitting its leash, enabling the dog to break free. The officers chased the dog, shooting at its silhouette in the dark, but continued to miss it. Instead, they shot the owner, who was trying to catch her pet, killing the woman.

Looking for Trouble

Between performances at Edinburgh's Fringe Festival, Oscar, a Labrador retriever billed as the world's only canine hypnotist, ran off. The owner told reporters to warn anyone seeing Oscar not to look him directly in the eye.

Lights Out

Urinating dogs in Tiburon, California, repeatedly shorted out a $20,000 sidewalk lighting system, costing the town $200 a month. The public works director, Tony Iacoppi, said canines can't resist the foot-tall lights, which illuminate the downtown Shoreline Park walkway. "All it takes is one dog to pee on it and then it's over," he said. "Every dog in the world wants to pee on them. They are corroding all the fixtures and all the wiring."

Cork It

A buildup of methane from 72 flatulent pigs in the hold of a South African Airways jet set off fire alarms, forcing the aircraft to turn back.

Watch Out Below

• Bob Ringewold was driving a rented car with his wife near Lake Michigan when he noticed an eagle flying overhead grasping a wriggling fish with its claws. "And then ka-bam," he said, explaining the five-pound fish slammed into the car's roof, leaving a considerable dent. Ringewold saved the dead fish as evidence and filed a police report, but the car-rental agent took his word, noting, "A person couldn't make up a story like that."

• After a hunter shot a six-pound goose in the Netherlands, it fell 75 feet, breaking the cheekbone of Anne Osinga, 60, chair of the Friesian Society for the Protection of Birds.

• Queen Elizabeth II was walking with guests at Balmoral Castle in the Scottish Highlands in 1995 when she was hit by a falling grouse, bruising her shoulder.

Warts and All

Toads overran three villages in central Bolivia for 10 days, causing widespread panic. Officials blamed a drought for forcing the toads from their usual habitats in search of water, but farmers reportedly took the invasion as a sign of impending doom. Children were described as terrified and unable to sleep. Radio dispatches said the main road connecting the region with La Paz was coated with a thick layer of dead toads, whose stench was unbearable.

Who's the Loony?

Cilicia H. Crawford, 25, was killed while trying to rescue a loon in the middle of the road in Tallahassee, Florida. The bird pecked her in the shin, causing her to jump back and hit a red Volkswagen Rabbit, according to Florida Highway Patrol Corporal T. L. Crawford, who said the victim fell and was run over by an oncoming car. The duck was unhurt. "The moral of the story," the officer said, "is leave the damn duck in the road."

More Than Just Pricks

The U.S. Forest Service officially closed the Rod and Gun Campground in South Dakota's Little Spearfish Canyon to protect campers from porcupines, which were discovered slipping under campers' vehicles and gnawing through brake lines to drink the brake fluid. "I assume a lot of petroleum products have salt content; that's generally what porcupines are looking for when they chew signs, buildings, paint, or anything like that," said Forest Service spokesperson Galen Roesler. "Obviously, if people get in their car in the morning and start down the canyon and suddenly don't have brakes, it's a real hazard."

Power Hungry

Toledo, Ohio, suffered a widespread power failure when millions of mayflies smothered an electrical generation plant. "No one has ever seen a swarm like that at the plant," a Toledo Edison official said.

Smoking Gun

A starling set fire to a three-bedroom house in Manchester, England, when it took a smoldering cigarette to its nest inside a wall in the house. Authorities said the ash from the cigarette ignited the nest, and the fire quickly spread.

We Take Care of Our Own

• After a schoolteacher shot a monkey that entered his garden in India's West Bengal state, the bleeding animal managed to drag itself to a nearby police station. After it was taken to a clinic, where it died, the body was returned to the station. Almost immediately, more than 50 other monkeys descended on the station and spent several hours outside shrieking.

• Some 60 monkeys attacked joggers and tourists at Malaysia's Penang Botanical Gardens after a young man stoned a baby monkey to death. The *New Straits Times* reported that since the man was wearing a yellow shirt, the monkeys attacked anyone wearing that color.

• When a man driving to work struck and killed a monkey in the Khamis Mesheit area of Saudi Arabia, other monkeys chased his car but couldn't catch him. According to the newspaper *Okaz*, when the man was returning from work later that day on the same highway, the monkeys were still gathered in the road around the corpse. They spotted his car and attacked it, breaking windows with their fists. The driver accelerated and escaped but said he saw the monkeys in his rear-view mirror dragging their slain companion into the mountains.

• Mokbul Kazi, a Bangladeshi farmer, tried to kill a snake in his home with a spear but only wounded it. The snake stuck to the mud and straw ceiling of the man's hut. That night, Kazi said some 50 snakes entered the hut, hissing loudly. He and his family fled, but the snakes remained for a week, leaving only when the wounded snake died.

School Daze

Officials investigating a three-alarm fire that caused $750,000 in damage to Vintage High School in Napa, California, blamed the blaze on an iguana. Napa Fire Department Captain Scott Sedgley said the reptile, which was kept in a cage in a science classroom, apparently knocked over a heat lamp, igniting nearby combustible material. Sedgley added it was the third fire he had heard of in the past five years caused by reptiles knocking over heat lamps.

Perils of Overfishing

After a 63-foot Norwegian fishing trawler netted a huge catch of herring, the crew tried to haul in the net, but the whole school swam for the bottom, capsizing the boat. Oslo's *Dagbladet* newspaper reported that panicked crew members tried to cut loose the net, but the vessel was sinking so fast the six of them had to abandon ship.

Hoover Monkeys

A pack of wild monkeys invaded the Japanese seaside resort of Ito, attacking at least 30 people. Twenty-six of the victims were women between the ages of 40 and 80. One monkey reportedly opened a door, entered the house, and bit Fukuyo Inaba, 62, on the ankle while she was vacuuming. The town responded by forming a "monkey patrol" armed with long sticks to guard the school. It also began broadcasting a warning over the loudspeaker system designed for earthquake alerts: "Monkeys are on the loose. If you go out, lock your door. Be cautious. Do not give them food."

Sugar, Sugar

As many as 100 baboons raided the local government hospital at Marsabit, northern Kenya, plucking dextrose fluid drips from terrified patients being treated for malaria and typhoid.

Happens Every Super Bowl

Keith Washington, 34, put his pet python in his bathtub to soak, then went to watch the Super Bowl at a neighbor's house in Chillicothe, Ohio. While he was away, the 12-foot snake apparently turned on a faucet, causing the bathtub to overflow and drip through to the apartment below.

Tool Time

A renegade deer that terrorized the Norwegian town of Aardalstangen for several weeks finally went too far when it used its antlers to pick up a chain saw from Olav Haereid's yard and ran off with it. The *Aarsal og Laerdal Avis* newspaper reported that the chain saw was so heavy, the deer managed to carry it only a few yards, but by then townspeople had had enough of the deer and shot it. "Sad, but we had no choice," forester Vidar Moen told the newspaper. "People were becoming frightened of the big animal."

It's Got a Gun!

• Four Iranian families picnicking outside Teheran were chasing a rabbit when they saw two snakes. One member of the party, 27-year-old Ali-Asghar Ahani, tried to trap one of the snakes alive by pressing it with the butt of his rifle. According to witnesses, the viper coiled around the weapon and pressed the trigger, causing the weapon to fire and kill Ali-Asghar.

• When Larry Lands of Potosi, Missouri, shot a turkey, he put it and his shotgun in the trunk of his car and drove to a neighbor's house. While his 16-year-old son was pulling the turkey he thought was dead out of the trunk, it began thrashing around. Its claw hit the trigger of the loaded shotgun, which fired through the side panel of the car, hitting Lands in the leg. To add insult to injury, Washington County Sheriff Ron Skiles said Lands faced a fine for hunting a week before the start of turkey season.

• Phillip Smith and John Phillips were hunting together near Inez, Kentucky, when Phillips's spaniel Rusty retrieved a downed bird. As Phillips tried to take the bird away, the dog stepped on the trigger of a 12-gauge shotgun and blasted Smith, 45, in both legs. "It's not funny that the guy got shot," Martin County Sheriff Darriel Young said, "but it's kind of funny how he got shot."

• Ernest Riddell, 56, was shot in the ankle while working in his auto repair shop in Kansas City, Kansas, when his cat pushed a loaded .22-caliber revolver off a workbench, causing it to fire.

• Joe Petrowski of Winnipeg, Manitoba, was home alone with his dog Vegas when he decided to fix the scope on his .22-caliber rifle. After mounting the gun on a workbench in his garage and shooting practice rounds at a target, he got up to check the target. A round remained in the chamber when Vegas apparently hit the trigger with her tail, shooting Petrowski in the back. Seriously wounded, he passed out, but Vegas revived him and pulled him to the house, where he phoned for help.

 **Appendix: Lists**

1. Private Zoos

In recent years animal control authorities and police agencies nationwide have encountered numerous cases of people hoarding animals in their homes. Professionals have dubbed them "animal warehousers" and say they suffer from "animal collector syndrome." For the most part, these folks are usually well intentioned in attempting to care for stray animals and their offspring. But as so often happens with people in these stories, situations tend to develop a life of their own and spiral out of control to a point where the caretakers are no longer capable of controlling them. What follows is a sampling of recent cases that have come to our attention.

• Jacksonport, Mississippi, 1991: One man living with 160 dogs and cats in his house, including dozens of cats living in his attic.

• Kingston, Ontario, 1992: Jack Wright, living with 600 cats in his house. Wearing a T-shirt reading ONE CAN NEVER HAVE TOO MANY CATS, Wright told reporters that he would continue to defy city laws requiring a six-cat-per-home limit and a licensing fee of $10 per cat. Wright said he spends $350 a day on cat food.

• Deltona, Florida, 1995: Angelo Russo, 79, living in

squalor with hundreds of rats. "I don't know what he had been feeding them, but these were nice big rats, fat and fluffy," environmental health official Paul Minshew said, adding, "I guess he'd bonded with them." The rats were so tame they just sat staring at health officials and exterminators, who killed more than 250 of the rodents. Hundreds more escaped or were left to die inside the walls and attic from poisoned bait.

• Winnipeg, Canada, 1992: An elderly man living in a house with 300 pet rats.

• Camas, Washington, 1993: A homeowner evicting a man from a house she owned found plastic bags and cardboard boxes filled with dead rats. Six kittens were packed in plastic Ziploc bags. The owner noted that it appeared some of the cats had been dead so long that the renter must have been moving them with him.

• Loudon County, Virginia, 1995: A couple in their early thirties living with more than 1,500 rats and mice in 130 cages, along with eight rabbits, eight snakes, two prairie dogs, and a hedgehog.

• Billings, Montana, 1996: Robert Dorton greeted authorities investigating complaints that he was keeping rats in his motel room by opening fire. Police and fire crews needed tear gas and a water cannon to subdue the man, who was seen kissing one of the rats and referred to them as "my brothers."

• Birmingham, Alabama, 1991: Norma Weakley, who called herself the "rat lady," lived with three dogs, five cats, and hundreds of rats in the backyard. She fed them Alpo beef chunks each day for dinner.

• Lantana, Florida, 1992: Darlene Cooper was accused of keeping 79 dogs (78 shar-peis and one German shepherd) in her home and conducting breeding experiments in hopes of creating a miniature shar-pei.

• St. Joseph, Missouri, 1992: A mother and son living in a house with almost a hundred exotic birds, including parrots, macaws, cockatoos, cockatiels and others.

• Hollywood, California, 1991: A woman who kept 33 cats and two dogs in a one-bedroom apartment and 45 cat corpses packed in the kitchen freezer, each wrapped in aluminum foil.

• Denver, Colorado, 1990: A woman who kept 138 cats in her home and 50 in someone else's house. "The stench coming from the ammonia was so bad," one police officer said, "that we had to wear gas masks to get into the house and collect the cats. We found feces all over the house. It was so bad that it covered the walls up to the light switches. Some of the cats had scratched their way through the walls."

• San Carlos, California, 1990: A couple living in a condominium with hundreds of pet rats. Forced to leave by the Department of Health, the woman tearfully said, "They took all of them. They weren't bothering anyone." Neighbors complained after they began seeing rats sitting in the couple's front windows, having eaten the curtains. As police entered the apartment they saw rats running everywhere, including lumps racing around underneath the bedcovers. The woman told authorities that the rats had the bedrooms and that she and her husband slept in the living room on a pull-out bed.

• East Topsham, Vermont, 1991: Three adults and two children sharing a 768-square-foot house with 155 dogs (14 of them pregnant), 14 cats, and 21 exotic birds. Three ponies, two calves, goats, and chickens roamed the yard. The owner of the home described the taking of his animals by police as "just like being in Russia." He said that his family sold dogs to make money. Hs wife claimed to regularly walk the dogs, saying, "I take them out on runs. We're working on building fences" for a dog run. After police described the filthy conditions in their house, including urine and feces everywhere, the couple claimed that the poop all came because of the raid. "They haven't had a chance to go to the bathroom," said the owner.

• Queens, New York, 1991: An elderly dog lover died of natural causes in her house. Investigators found her body about a week after her death. She had been eaten from the waist down by her 18 dogs.

• Scottsdale, Arizona, 1990: An elderly couple was found living with 75 dead cats, each packed in a toolbox. Six months before the discovery, the wife had been found staying in an area motel room with 71 sick cats.

• Camden, New Jersey, 1997: An adult and a teenager sharing a three-bedroom home with 20 dead cats and dogs, four kittens, two puppies, 11 adult cats, three adult dogs, and two rabbits.

• Tampa, Florida, 1997: A 76-year-old woman and her 54-year-old daughter living in a house with 1,200 rats. "To be honest," the daughter said, "we didn't notice them."

• Toulouse, France, 1996: An elderly woman living with 1,000 rats and some cats. She slept on the floor surrounded by the cats and fed the rats 33 pounds of grain per day.

• Los Angeles, California, 1995: A woman living in a house with 38 potbellied pigs. "She seems to love them dearly," an animal warden said, "but it just got away from her."

• Elgin, New Jersey, 1993: Firefighters responding to a burning mobile home found a refrigerator full of dead cats. The corpses numbered more than 50. Some were wrapped in trash bags and food storage bags, and dead kittens were in cans. Police estimate that some of the cats had been frozen for 10 years. The owner of the home lived there alone.

2. Look What the Cat/Dog Dragged In

• New Caney, Texas, 1990: A dog brought home a severed human hand. A month later he brought home a second severed hand, apparently the mate of the first one.

• Southport, Florida, 1990: A dog brought home shoes containing decomposing human feet. They led to the discovery of two dead people in a submerged car.

• Waukegan, Illinois, 1995: A dog found one leg in the woods and five days later brought home the second leg. Police failed to find a body but noted that the legs had been sawed off.

• Waterloo, New York, 1989: A dog brought home a human skull, which police said had been buried for some time.

• East St. Louis, Missouri, 1991: Two dogs found a skull in their backyard. The body was found two blocks away.

• Fort Lauderdale, Florida, 1990: A dog playing fetch with its owners near a river jumped in to retrieve a stick and returned with a bag containing a severed head and two arms.

3. Wanderlust

• Pine Bluff, Arkansas, 1997: A cat named Shadow traveled 90 miles in 10 days to get home.

• Central Islip, New York, 1995: Buddy, a German shepherd missing for four days, was found 1,600 miles away in Fort Collins, Colorado.

• Marseille, France, 1995: Chippie the cat walked the length of the French Riviera, from her new home in Marseille to her old home in Nice.

• Beaver Dam, Wisconsin, 1991: The owners of a cat named Sam moved the family from Wisconsin to Arizona in 1986. In 1987 they returned to Wisconsin, leaving Sam behind in Arizona. Four years later, the cat returned to the old homestead in Wisconsin, having traveled 1,400 miles.

• Copenhagen, Denmark, 1995: A kitten named Venus disappeared but was returned to her owner by an animal shelter that found her 11 years later, 160 miles from where she disappeared.

• Grinnell, Iowa, 1995: Pete, a German short-haired pointer, traveled 1,500 miles from Iowa to Oregon.

• Lyde, England, 1995: Chester the tortoise turned up in its old neighborhood 35 years after it disappeared. Malcom Edwards, 44, identified his long-lost pet by a paint mark made on its shell by his father.

 **Sources**

Agence France-Press
Albuquerque Journal
Argus Leader (Sioux Falls, South Dakota)
Arizona Daily News
Arlington Journal (Virginia)
Asahi Evening News
Associated Press
Atlanta Journal Constitution
Austin American-Statesman
Bangkok Post
Beacon Journal (Akron, Ohio)
Belleville News-Democrat (Illinois)
Birmingham News
The Boston Globe
Boston Herald
Casper Star Tribune (Wyoming)
Chicago Tribune
China Post
Cincinnati Enquirer
Columbus Dispatch (Ohio)
Courier-Mail (Brisbane, Australia)
Crescent News (Defiance, Ohio)
Democrat and Chronicle (Rochester, New York)
Denver Post

Des Moines Register
Dog World
Edmonton Journal (Canada)
Edmonton Sun (Canada)
The European
Fortean Times
Gainesville Sun (Florida)
Gannett News Service
Globe & Mail (Toronto, Canada)
Houston Chronicle
Kansas City Star (Missouri)
Knight-Ridder News Service
Knoxville Journal (Tennessee)
The Knoxville News-Sentinel (Tennessee)
Lafayette Journal-Courier (Indiana)
Los Angeles Daily News
Los Angeles Times
The Miami Herald
Minneapolis Star Tribune
Montreal Journal
Morning Call (Allentown, Pennsylvania)
Nairobi Times
Nanaimo Times (Canada)
Naples Daily News (Florida)
Nation (Pakistan)
New Scientist
New York Daily News
New York Post
The New York Times
News-Press/Gazette (St. Joseph, Missouri)
Newsweek
Olympian (Washington)
The Orlando Sentinel (Florida)
Ottawa Citizen
Palm Beach Post (Florida)
Philadelphia Daily News

The Philadelphia Inquirer
Pittsburgh Post-Gazette
Pittsburgh Press
The Post-Standard (Syracuse, New York)
Reading Eagle (Pennsylvania)
Reuters
Rocky Mountain News (Denver, Colorado)
Sacramento Union (California)
Saginaw News (Michigan)
St. Louis Post-Dispatch
St. Petersburg Times (Florida)
San Francisco Chronicle
San Jose Mercury News (California)
Scranton Tribune (Pennsylvania)
Scripps Howard News Service
Seattle Times
Standard-Times (New Bedford, Massachusetts)
The Star-Ledger (Newark, New Jersey)
State (Columbia, South Carolina)
The Sun (Baltimore, Maryland)
Syracuse Herald-Journal (New York)
Texas Monthly
Time
The Times (London, England)
The Times-Picayune (New Orleans, Louisiana)
Toronto Star
Toronto Sun
Tuscaloosa News (Alabama)
United Press International
USA Today
U.S. News & World Report
The Wall Street Journal
The Washington Post
The Washington Times
World Press Review
Yorkshire Post (England)